Preaching and Culture in Latino Congregations

PREACHING AND CULTURE IN LATINO CONGREGATIONS

Edited by Kenneth G. Davis
and Jorge L. Presmanes

LITURGY
TRAINING
PUBLICATIONS

This book was conceived and the essays gathered by Kenneth G. Davis and Jorge L. Presmanes. With the exception of the essays by Rosa María Icaza and Jorge Presmanes, all of the articles were also published in the fall/winter 2000 issue of *Chicago Studies*. The editors thank that journal and the Civitas Dei Foundation for granting the right to republish those articles. We also wish to thank the ACTA Foundation for their financial support of this project. This kind aid was provided under the auspices of the Instituto de Liturgia Hispana. We are indebted to its executive director, Doris Turek, SSND.

The diagram on page 105 is used with the permission of Dr. Marina Herrera.

We are grateful to the photographers and archivists who have granted permission to reprint their work. Every attempt has been made to determine the copyright holders and to make proper arrangements to use these images. Any oversight, if brought to our attention, will be gladly corrected in future printings.

We dedicate this book to Saints Dominic and Francis, great preachers whose spiritual children brought the Good News to the New World.

PREACHING AND CULTURE IN LATINO CONGREGATIONS © 2000 Archdiocese of Chicago: Liturgy Training Publications, 1800 North Hermitage Avenue, Chicago IL 60622-1101; 1-800-933-1800; fax 1-800-933-7094; orders@ltp.org; www.ltp.org. All rights reserved.

Visit our website at www.ltp.org.

Leo Lefebure, the editor of *Chicago Studies*, did the final preparation of this manuscript for publication. Audrey Novak Riley was the production editor. The design is by M. Urgo and the typesetting was done by Mark Hollopeter in Palatino. This book was printed by Webcom in Toronto, Canada. The cover art is by Guillermo Delgado.

ISBN 1-56854-363-8
PCLAT

Contents

Kenneth G. Davis, OFM CONV

Introduction:
Chiles in the Melting Pot

The melting pot metaphor continues to bubble despite the efforts of decades to put a lid on it. The heat under the metaphorical pot is the obviously absurd but perpetually tantalizing insistence that Hispanics, like every other "immigrant" group before them, will all be boiled into a gray, tasteless mash within a generation. From this premise one argues that it is therefore fruitless to learn about any specific spices they may bring to the pot. Anyone who bothers to learn their language or culture will only become the heir of anachronism.

I suggest the opposite: namely, that the power of Hispanic cultures and the strength of their numbers is like adding bushels of *chiles* to the melting pot; they will forever change the flavor of everything in U.S. society. Preachers must understand that there are historic reasons why Hispanics will not assimilate and contemporary explanations for their growing influence on all society.

Historically, the Hispanic presence in our country is distinct from that of Western Europeans. First, they were the first! The Catholic church in the United States did not begin in Baltimore and rush west. Rather, it began in Puerto Rico, moved to Florida, and was strung like a rosary along the rivers of the Southwest and up the coast of California. Some of those original beads continue to shine with ecclesial life. Unlike last century's immigrants from Europe, many Hispanic Catholics can trace their family's heritage in this country to a time before Jamestown. Thus, especially for Mexican Americans, many did not immigrate into the United States; rather, emigrants from the United States moved into and eventually seized territory that was Mexican or Spanish.

Second, even new Hispanic immigrants need not abandon their culture. Unlike the waves of European immigrants, they have had no ocean to cross, only a small river or the Gulf Stream. Thus a steady flow of compatriots is always renewing the language and culture.

Third, unlike previous generations, technology now allows emigrants to make telephone calls to family at home, receive print, radio, television and Internet information from their country of origin or fly home for holidays. This means that even Hispanics who do not live in their own large enclaves can still remain in touch with their ethnic roots.

Fourth, despite their historical lack of clergy, Hispanics have always maintained their own vibrant and unique spiritualities through popular religion, that is, devotions and religious beliefs that constitute them as a people. These symbols have been in the hands of the laity, especially women, and are as enduring as cacti in the desert.

Fifth, since the civil rights movement, both society in general and ethnic enclaves in particular have been more accepting of acculturation rather than assimilation. Acculturation is the negotiation of two cultures such that one person belongs to more than one culture. Although Hispanic children often idealize assimilation, by the time they begin forming personal identities in high school, they learn to navigate both home and host cultures without rejecting either.

Sixth, outside of television, Hispanics tend to have darker skin than Europeans. Hispanics, especially Afro-Latinos, experience racism. This external pressure helps maintain separation rather than promoting assimilation between Hispanics (who may be of any race) and their whiter neighbors.

These are historic reasons why Hispanics will not only continue to resist assimilation as they have, but will actually exert increasing influence over the rest of U.S. society. There are also more contemporary explanations.

Emigration from Spanish-speaking countries will remain high. The U.S. economy, strong as it is, depends on cheap foreign labor. And Latin American economies generally do not provide enough employment for all the employable. As long as people need to eat, they will move to where they can earn food for themselves and their children.

Emigration from Latin America affects not only the receiving nation, but also the country of origin. For generations virtually only men immigrated to the United States from Mexico, for instance. This meant that the women left at home had to embrace occupations and roles previously reserved for men. These changing roles for women are one of the reasons they now are also emigrating. Moreover, as dollars flood the local economies, inflation results. Soon families become dependent upon money from the United States not simply to supplement their income or enable their economic advancement, but for survival. Thus the pressures to emigrate are always mounting.

Government interventions on both sides of the border have often had the unintended consequence of increasing emigration as well. Despite Mexico's natural riches, periodic pronouncements that it will soon export products and not people have never materialized. Civil strife, abusive governments and draconian economic policies (often imposed or supported by the United States), are behind the massive emigration from Spanish-speaking countries other than Mexico.

The United States has also contributed to the increase of immigration and the change in its characteristic. The Immigration Reform and Control Act of 1986 and related measures to curtail benefits to immigrants and their children were both morally questionable and decidedly unsuccessful. Over 4.5 million seasonal immigrants who used to return to Mexico each year have now settled in the United States in order to regularize their status here. And all the fences and vigilantism along the border have only driven Hispanics from that region into the heartland of the country. Open the *National Catholic Reporter* almost any week: Dioceses that twenty years ago did not even have a Taco Bell are advertising to fill Hispanic ministry positions.

But immigration alone will not account for the fact that Hispanics in the United States will soon outnumber African Americans. The high birth rate of the very youthful Latino/a population is another reason for their rising numbers. And this very youthfulness will insure that like immigration, high births among Hispanics will continue to increase their numbers.

Hispanics *qua* Hispanics are here to stay. And the *chile, casabe* and *arepas* they add to the melting pot will not lose their flavor, but rather will slowly change the tastes of U.S. society.

Latino voting power is rising and being recognized. Now 7 percent of voters nationally, they can already swing elections in such electorally important states as New York, California, Florida and Texas. Perhaps that is why the Democratic Party elected Lydia Camarillo to serve as president of their convention for the year 2000. Businesses are not only recognizing the burgeoning economic clout of Hispanics, but are marketing traditionally Hispanic products to the rest of society. Salsa now outsells catsup. Ricky Martin, Cristina Aguilera, Marc Anthony and Jennifer Lopez are only a few of the Hispanic stars reaching audiences of non-Hispanics. Sammy Sosa is but one household word in sports. The cultural penetration of Hispanics is slow but inevitable. When Hispanics marry outside their culture or join churches not traditionally associated with them, they are influenced by and also influence the new peoples with whom they interact. The melting pot is not just changing Hispanics; Hispanics are changing the composition and flavor of the pot itself.

How ought Catholic preachers in the United States respond to the unprecedented change in this bubbling stew? That is the question posed to each of the authors in this collection. While none offers a simplistic recipe, each samples this new taste, comments on a color or texture, and helps the preacher appreciate and communicate these new elements brought to our eucharistic banquet.

To a great extent the future of the church will depend upon reaching this cusp community and raising up preachers and witnesses among them. So we gather here historic and contemporary reflections on preaching within this community that for contemporary and historic reasons will inevitably season and strengthen our U.S. Catholic church. I invite you to open the lid, breathe the steamy aromas, contemplate the swirl of colors, and savor this healthy new brew. Taste and see the goodness of the Lord!

Jorge L. Presmanes, OP

The Juxtaposition of Dangerous Memories: Toward a Latino Theology of Preaching from the Underside of the Diaspora Experience

Painful and dangerous memories of exile and otherness, when united to preaching the message of Jesus, can serve as powerful catalysts of transformation of the world.

INTRODUCTION

The theology of liturgical preaching presented here is grounded in the contemporary cultural context of Latino men and women whose lives have been marked by the exilic experience of diaspora. The hermeneutical framework for this theology of preaching has two components: first, the collective narrative of the diaspora experience of Latinos, which is characterized by a profound alienation and a pervasive sense of otherness; and second, the collective narrative of the Christian community as it gathers at liturgy to keep the memory of the paschal mystery. I argue that the Latino community's memories of otherness and exile, when juxtaposed with the memories of the paschal event at the liturgy, become a self-defining and liberating experience for the community.

This theology of preaching is based on four theological concepts. First, a theology of revelation asserting that God is revealed in human experience, which thus renders the cultural context of the faithful not only a social location and source for theology, but also a privileged source of revelation. Second, a recognition that the encounter between the tradition of faith and the culture of the local church, often referred to as inculturation, is central to the development of a sound liturgical theology of preaching. Third, an understanding that liturgy is always informed by culture and is indelibly marked by the worshiping community's history. Fourth, a belief that universal truth is found in the particularity of culture.

I begin with a description of the Latino diaspora experience that encompasses three perspectives: personal, collective and theological, including a discussion of the role that the "dangerous memory" plays in the liberation process. Subsequently, the topic of liturgy as memorial and locus for the juxtaposition of memories is explored. In the final section, a Latino theology of preaching is presented. Recognizing that all preaching contains both explicit and implicit christologies, ecclesiologies and spiritualities, I will delineate elements of each of these theological categories from the perspective of the experience of otherness of the Latino diaspora. I will also offer some practical suggestions and possible preaching metaphors that might be helpful in preaching in the midst of this graced community.

THE CENTRALITY OF THE ASSEMBLY

In the NCCB document, *Fulfilled in Your Hearing: The Homily in the Sunday Assembly,* the authors insist that any treatment of the Sunday homily has to begin with the "assembly rather than with the preacher or homily" (Washington: United States Catholic Conference [1982], 3–4). To begin with the assembly is to enter into the complexities of the life, dreams and hopes of a people, to delve into the concreteness of their culture and to theologize from this unique and privileged source of revelation. The encounter between the tradition of faith and the culture of the local church is the methodological axis of the theology of preaching presented here: a theology from below that is grounded in the cultural context of the people who comprise the liturgical assembly.

There are many elements of the culture that could be used as the hermeneutical grounding for theological reflection. Drawing on my personal history, as well as the self-articulated experiences of the Latinos whom I have ministered to and with for almost twenty years, I will use the experience of alienation and otherness that we all share as theological source and social location. Obviously, each of us Latinos has experienced alienation and otherness in different ways and to different degrees. Yet we are all marked by these memories that form our collective narrative. As I will illustrate throughout this article, there is extraordinary power in our memories of otherness and exile; for when they are juxtaposed to the memories of the Christian narrative in the liturgy, they become memories that act as a catalyst both to transform us and to move us to become agents of transformation in the world.

THE LATINO DIASPORA EXPERIENCE AS SOCIAL LOCATION FOR THEOLOGICAL REFLECTION

The classic definition of a diaspora is "a dispersion of an originally homogeneous people" (*The New American Heritage Dictionary*, Second College Edition [Boston: Houghton Mifflin, 1982]). Yet this definition does not do justice to the reality of what we Latinos have experienced. The experience of diaspora is multivalent. It is a place of alienation where a sense of radical otherness is experienced as a way of life. When I was nine years old and unable to speak a word of English, I boarded a plane in Havana bound for Miami. When it landed after the forty-minute flight, my life was forever changed, for I was now other. Let me illustrate the phenomenon of otherness. Two years after my arrival in the United States, I became a member of the Boy Scouts of America in Hialeah, Florida. One night when I arrived early at one of our troop meetings, six or seven of the boys already there were involved in a spirited discussion about the evils of the Cubans who were taking over the neighborhood. I stood there, unbeknownst to them, listening to the hatred that was rendering me null and void. One of my "friends" turned around at one point and saw me standing in their midst. The nervous silence that followed was broken when one of them said: "Oh, but you're different." In retrospect, I realize that they were right. I was different, not from my Cuban brothers and sisters, but from them. I was other to them.

Another experience of otherness occurred when I returned to Cuba to visit my father and the rest of my family. On Sunday, the entire clan gathered for a midday meal followed by a lively exchange on the socio-political and economic situation of Cuba today. In an attempt to participate in the discussion, I voiced my views on the topic at hand. Out of hospitality, I was graciously allowed to complete my thoughts. But then my own brother said: "You have no idea what we go through every day. You are an American." I was left speechless at the realization that I was other to them as well and thus homeless—a foreigner in the land of my exile as well as in the land that gave me birth.

Diaspora is the experience of being rendered other. This otherness may have its roots in being a person from one country and culture living in another, as in my case. However, it is not limited to being an exile or an expatriate (Fernando Segovia, "Toward a Hermeneutics of the Diaspora: Hermeneutics of Otherness and Engagement," *Reading from This Place: Social Location and Biblical Interpretation in the United States* [Minneapolis: Fortress Press, 1995], 60). The diaspora of otherness is experienced by women in a patriarchal society, by gay men and lesbian women in a heterosexist social milieu, by African Americans in a culture of racism, and by people with disabilities in a world that continually limits their access and mobility. Each experience of diaspora is unique. Even the experience of diaspora of Latinos in the United States is not a homogenous one. The experience of otherness that an Afro-Cuban American encounters in this country varies from that faced by a white Cuban American. And the experience of otherness of a Latino who stayed in this country after completing his or her doctoral degree at an American university is different from what a migrant worker experiences. Yet what we all share is the radical otherness that flows from being strangers in the Latin American countries of our heritage and aliens in the land where we live. This twofold experience of otherness is the crux of the Latino diaspora, and the hermeneutical key and social location of this theology of preaching.

For me, as an eleven-year-old boy, experiencing the bestowal of other at a Boy Scout meeting was without a doubt an overwhelming incident. What eleven-year-old wants to be rendered different from his or her peers? At the time, my response was to internalize the hatred. I managed, with great effort, to rid myself of that accent that so marked my otherness, and "Jorge" became "George." Segovia would define this as the "classic pattern of the colonized—passivity, submission, obedience" (64). It took a decade before I was able to free myself of a colonized mentality and experience my otherness as constructive self-identity, the vehicle by which I could become the author of my own history and destiny.

The experience of being other can be life-giving or death-dealing; it can be liberating or debilitating. It is life-giving and liberating when I embrace it as a rich and wonderful gift of God and use it as a source of my self-identity. It is death-dealing and oppressive when it is imposed on me, as was my experience at the Boy Scout troop meeting in Miami and the family reunion in Havana. We in the Latino diaspora can allow the experience of otherness to define our identity or deprive us of our identity. I choose the former, and in so doing my otherness becomes my voice. "From such a voice," Segovia writes, "emerges a profound commitment not to overwhelm or override the other but rather to acknowledge it, value it, engage it—a theology of mixture and otherness, a hermeneutics of otherness and engagement" (67).

THE DANGEROUS MEMORY OF THE DIASPORA

In *Faith in History and Society*, Johann Baptist Metz writes about the "dangerous memory" as an instrument of liberation (New York: Crossroad, 1980). Sharon Welch, building on Metz's work, holds that memories of marginalization and oppression are painful recollections that "become dangerous when they are used as the foundation for a critique of existing institutions and ideologies that blur the recognition and denunciation of injustice" (*Feminist Ethic of Risk* [Minneapolis: Fortress, 1990], 154–55). Dangerous memories are intensely powerful because they have the ability to impel those who have been rendered powerless to act. For us Latinos, the memories of otherness, of being pushed to the margins, of being silenced, of alienation and oppression, are indeed dangerous because they are memories that have transformed many of us into the authors of our own destiny and agents of change in society.

The diaspora experience of Latinos is replete with dangerous memories. For example, in 1985 I entered the Southern Dominican Province novitiate. An integral part of the experience for all men and women novices was to participate in the Dominican inter-novitiate program. A presentation was made by a well-known Dominican historian on the history of the Dominican Order in the United States. The interesting presentation began with Edward Dominic Fenwick, OP, who founded the St. Joseph Dominican Province in Springfield, Kentucky, in 1806. At the end of the presentation, I asked the historian why she began the history of the Dominicans in the United States with Fenwick, when in fact there were Hispanic Dominicans present and even martyred (for example, Luis Cancer, OP, in Florida in 1549) in what is now the United States more than 250 years before Fenwick's arrival. Her quick and acerbic response was that this information was "insignificant to Dominican history today." Her abrupt end to the conversation translated to "you and your history are other and insignificant to us, so shut up and stay in your place."

The memory of being publicly rendered silent and voiceless has been for me a transformative experience. Its transformative character has been twofold. First, being silenced has given me the courage to fight for a voice for myself and for my Latino brothers and sisters. Second, it has made me sensitive to others who are systematically rendered silent in our society and has made me aware that I also have a hand in their silencing. It is essentially because of this transformative and liberating impact on the keeper of the memory that the memory is dangerous. In other words, the memories of otherness become liberating when they are turned into the vehicle for claiming the voice that has been rendered silent (Segovia, 64). This has been my experience and the experience of many of my Latino brothers and sisters. It is, however, with great caution that I claim that my dangerous memories of marginalization and oppression are paradigmatic of the diaspora experience of Latinos. I say it cautiously because I, as a Caucasian middle-class priest with a privileged education, have suffered infinitely less than most of my brothers and sisters in the Latino diaspora.

INCULTURATED THEOLOGIES: THE PROCESS OF FINDING UNIVERSAL TRUTH IN THE PARTICULARITY OF CULTURE

To ground a theology of preaching in the cultural context of a people is of great value, not just to make preaching pertinent and interesting to the hearers of the proclamation, but because the cultural context itself is a privileged source of revelation. The theological endeavor is about discerning and articulating the faith tradition of the church. A wellspring for discerning this tradition is the *sensus fidelium* (sense of the faithful). This is a theological source because it is the fruit of the Spirit active in the church. Orlando Espín claims that the *sensus fidelium* is a privileged source of revelation, "because the foundational origin of the *sensus fidelium* is the Holy Spirit." He further states that "this 'sense of the faithful' is infallible, preserved by the Spirit from error in matters necessary to revelation" ("Tradition and Popular Religion: An Understanding of the *Sensus Fidelium*," in *Frontiers of Hispanic Theology in the United States*, ed. Allan F. Deck [New York: Orbis, 1992], 65).

This Spirit-filled "sense of the faithful" is a particular reality of great universal value. It is particular in the sense that it is concrete; that is to say, it is the expression of the faith of a local church. It is of universal value because the praxis of faith of a local church holds part of the universal truth that the theological community is in search of and attempting to articulate. Because it is guided by the Spirit of Truth, the faith experience of a particular and local church contains within it a "unique mystery of absolutely universal value" (Yves Congar, "Christianity and Faith and Culture," *East Asian Pastoral Review* 18/4 [1981]: 304). Thus, the *sensus fidelium* is a rich Spirit-filled fountain for theology contextualized in the particular, but yielding part of a universal truth. Given that contextualized or inculturated theologies, like the one presented here, are grounded in the particular experience of the local church, they become vehicles by which a plurality of voices in the church can be heard. They provide access to many who have been silenced in the past or whose voices have been omitted from the theological debate, to the detriment of the church and of the theological community.

LITURGY AS MEMORIAL AND LOCUS FOR THE JUXTAPOSITION OF DANGEROUS MEMORIES

Liturgy can be defined as "the symbolic articulation of the Christian community's relationship with God" (James Empereur, *Exploring the Sacred* [Washington: Pastoral Press, 1987], viii). Inculturated liturgical theology uses the experience of a particular community's relationship with God, articulated in symbolic and metaphorical activity in worship, as a liturgical source. This understanding of worship expands the horizon of liturgical text, the primary source of liturgical theology, to include context (Kevin Irwin, "Method in Liturgical Theology: Context is Text," *Église et Théologie* 20 [1989], and *Context as Text* [Collegeville: Liturgical Press, 1995]).

In his article on the hermeneutics of the diaspora experience, Segovia argues that a new "flesh and blood" reader must be introduced in the praxis of biblical criticism. By this he means that in biblical criticism the context of the reader of the text is inseparable from the text itself. The introduction of the "flesh and blood" reader in biblical criticism, he argues, acknowledges that "no reading, informed or uninformed, takes place in a social vacuum or desert" (Segovia, 57). Like biblical criticism, liturgy and its preaching do not take place in a vacuum. It is a concrete community that is praying the text and hearing the proclamation, in a particular place and moment in history. To introduce the Latino "flesh and blood" worshiper as source and text for liturgical theology is to "decolonize" the church and liberate a theology "that has been, from the beginning to end and top to bottom, thoroughly Eurocentric despite its assumed scientific persona of neutrality and universality" (Segovia, 57). As the "irruption of the flesh and blood reader" is a liberating experience for the discipline of biblical criticism, so also the irruption of the "flesh and blood" worshiper is liberating for liturgical theology.

The liturgical theology of preaching presented here holds that liturgy is memorial or anamnesis when it is invoked by the texts (the ancient text being prayed and the "flesh and blood" text that is doing the praying) through the juxtaposition of metaphors, symbols and the elements of the ordo. For the Latino community, what is invoked by these texts is the memory of a God who has been irrevocably committed to God's people throughout history, and specifically throughout the exile experience of the Latino diaspora. This irrevocable commitment to solidarity with those rendered other has been made manifest through the life, death and resurrection of Jesus Christ.

The keeper of the memory of the Christ event is the liturgical community in its present reality. Richard Schaeffler argues that the present is the home where the remembered past and hoped-for future combine in the liturgy. This juxtaposition occurs not in some "abstract act of thought or in the pure interiority of imagination," but rather by entering into a "correlative relationship with God" that renders God's saving memories of the past effective in the present. ("Therefore We Remember . . . " *The Meaning of the Liturgy*, ed. Angelus A. Haussling [Collegeville: The Liturgical Press, 1994], 15). Thus, from the social location of the Latino diaspora, the salvific act of the paschal mystery which is remembered in the liturgy becomes effectively present when the memory of Jesus' otherness embracing humanness is juxtaposed with the memories of our life of exile, when the memory of the suffering and death of Jesus is juxtaposed with the memories of the death and suffering of the experience of otherness of our community, and when the memory of the resurrection of Christ is juxtaposed with our dreams and hopes for a new order in society in which otherness and exile no longer exist.

The effectiveness of the soteriological event that is made present in the liturgy is found in the conversion of the keeper of the memory, in the transformation of the Christian who dies with Christ to sin to be born anew for God in Christ Jesus (Romans 6:11). The passage from death to life is mediated by the anamnesis of the liturgy when "the remembered past and anticipated future . . . are gathered up in the present celebration" (Schaeffler, 31). The anamnetic juxtapositions of the life, death and hope-filled resurrection of Jesus Christ with the dangerous memories of the diaspora is the catalyst for transformation. Thus, through the church's liturgical event, memories of defeat are transmuted into hopeful anticipation. In other words, the dangerous memories of otherness and exile help us

define our identity as Latinos; the dangerous memories of the paschal mystery help us define our identity as baptized Christians; the
juxtaposition of the two in the liturgy helps us define our identity as
agents of transformation for the world and gives us hope for a new
dawn of justice in the future.

A CHRISTOLOGICAL PERSPECTIVE FROM
THE UNDERSIDE OF THE LATINO DIASPORA

All authentic Christian theologies of preaching are incarnate. They
presuppose that in Jesus Christ, God is revealed in history, in culture
and in human experience. Not only is God revealed in history, but
also in Jesus Christ, God becomes one with the oppressed, with
those who have been reduced to being other, with those cast aside
and silenced by society. This Latino theology of preaching is
grounded on a Christology that takes heed of Jesus' solidarity with
the oppressed and calls for such solidarity in the here and now.

The preacher in the Latino community struggles with the word
of God to embrace the hermeneutical bias in favor of the oppressed.
He or she goes to the scriptures bearing in mind the whole experience of otherness and exile of Latinos and looks for the hope and the
grace being revealed in the ancient texts as well as the living texts of
the Latino diaspora. In the Latino community, the preacher does not
repeat the tradition in his or her preaching but transforms the tradition. He or she does not go back to the ancient world to find answers
to unique 21st-century problems, but rather seeks divine truth by
struggling with the implications of the juxtaposition of the ancient
text with the contemporary text that is the experience of the worshiping community. The preaching is the grace-filled fruit of this
evangelical struggle.

The anamnetic juxtaposition of the dangerous memories of the
paschal mystery with the diaspora has led the Latino community,
by contrast experience, to formulate a Christology and a corresponding ecclesiology of inclusion. By contrast experience I am
referring to what appears as the absence of God in the painful experience of otherness. Yet, because we hold firm to a God of radical
compassion and solidarity with the oppressed as revealed by Jesus
Christ, we know to be fact that the experience of marginality is the

antithesis to Jesus' preaching, in word and deed, of the Reign of God (Mary Catherine Hilkert, *Naming Grace: Preaching and the Sacramental Imagination* [New York: Continuum, 1998], 54).

The Reign of God as radical inclusion is illustrated by Jesus' ministerial praxis on behalf of the oppressed. It is also revealed in the summoning of the Twelve. In the Markan account, Jesus "called to him those whom he desired; and they came to him . . . to be with him, and to be sent out to preach and . . . to cast out demons" (Mark 3:13–14). In this narrative, Jesus then calls the Twelve by name. He brings together in community Matthew the "tax collector" with Simon the "Zealot" and Peter the "rock" with Judas the "traitor." He brings together in community twelve men who are all very different from each other. What unites them is faith in Jesus and the mission of proclaiming the Reign of God in word ("to preach") and deed ("to cast out demons"). Why would Jesus bring such diverse individuals together instead of calling people of common backgrounds and like minds? I argue that it was a strategic decision. He wanted the preaching of the Reign of God to be heard and embraced by all. What better way was there for a diverse group of people to embrace his message than to hear it proclaimed by a diverse group of preachers living together in community?

This theology of preaching sees the Latino people of God as a community that preaches the Reign of God as a place of hope, rich in diversity and absent the oppressive contrast experience of being silenced and of being rendered other. The preaching that arises from this theology reminds the Christian community that it is, like the community of the Twelve, a community united in their commitment of faith and mission. The faith is in Jesus Christ. The mission is the continuation of his mission: to preach, in word and deed, the Reign of God, that hoped-for place of radical inclusiveness. For us Latinos who by our experience of diaspora have been excluded and made to feel homeless, the Reign of God as home is a powerful image.

POLITICS IN THE PULPIT OF THE LATINO COMMUNITY

Latino preaching rejects the spirituality that has too often been preached from pulpits in our church, the spirituality that equates the religious journey with the "cultivation of individualistic values as a way to personal perfection" (Gustavo Gutiérrez, *We Drink from Our Own Wells* [Maryknoll: Orbis, 1985], 14). What is rejected here is a spirituality that encourages Christians to be self-absorbed in their own interiority and to see the Christian life as the development of individualistic virtues that are totally disconnected from social change. Though this spirituality is highly attractive to Christians in a therapeutic culture, it is inconsistent with the missiological endeavor of the church. Thus, this Latino theology of preaching challenges overly subjective Christian preaching and proposes a Christian praxis that is linked to social context and that in turn advocates systemic change.

Preaching that perpetuates a spirituality focused solely on the conversion of the individual betrays the dangerous memories of the diaspora experience. Our experience of oppression and marginalization leads us to the conclusion that injustice and oppression spring from the history of a society. Therefore, while no one is individually responsible for oppression, everyone has a hand in it. If change for a more just and less oppressive way is to be actualized, then what is needed is to convert the system or institution from which oppression springs. And because all individuals have a hand in it, they also must change. However, the view that the system will change when people are converted is a fallacy. Preaching in the Latino community must be a catalyst for both individual and systemic conversion (*National Pastoral Plan for Hispanic Ministry*, 56).

There are many people in the Christian community who believe that politics has no place in the pulpit. To those people, the preacher who grounds his or her preaching in human experience must point to the fact that "political life is so all-pervasive in human experience that to expurgate any reference to it" from the preaching can only move preaching to the margins of society where it is irrelevant (James Empereur, *Models of Liturgical Theology* [Nottingham: Grove, 1987], 41).

Not only is preaching irrelevant when it fails to address political issues that greatly affect the community and the building-up of the Reign of God, but also it becomes the right hand of the perpetuation of oppression. Justo and Catherine Gonzalez pose the question: "Why is it that in so much preaching and teaching in the church 'sin' is usually equated with an inner attitude, or at best with private misdeeds, and so seldom with the sort of sin most often condemned in the Bible?" They underline the fact that much too often in Christian preaching, sin is equated with "sexual disorders, while ignoring social injustice." Their hermeneutics of suspicion leads them to the conclusion that the reason this occurs is that "once again and quite unwittingly, Christian theology has been serving the interests of the powerful" (Justo and Catherine Gonzalez, *Liberation Preaching: The Pulpit and the Oppressed* [Nashville: Abingdon, 1980], 41). The Latino theology of preaching presented here stands within the ancient Christian tradition. However, the experience of oppression or of being in solidarity with the oppressed leads the preacher in the Latino community to approach the tradition with the suspicion that arises when one realizes that the gospel, and its preaching, has been in the hands of dominant groups for too long. With the knowledge that the tradition has been dominated by the powerful, the preacher in solidarity with those who have been rendered other, must be open to "modify, change or even reject those traditions based on new experiences" (Mary Catherine Hilkert, "Naming Grace: A Theology of Proclamation," *Worship* 60 [September 1986]: 444).

From the experience of marginality of the diaspora, the preacher in the Latino community preaches justice. But the preacher of justice must be careful not to induce personal guilt in the worshiper. Many preachers live in the security of a middle-class existence and often feel personally guilty for having a privileged status in society. Often, as a result of preaching justice, preachers project their own sense of guilt onto their congregations as if they and their congregations chose to be born into a privileged class. The guilt being denounced here is personal guilt attached to individual action. No one individual is responsible for oppressive structures. Feeling personally guilty about such things is counter-productive to the active and concrete effort to change death-dealing structures.

If we turn to the experience of the diaspora and its corresponding dangerous memories for insight, we find that instead of personal guilt, preachers must embrace their own reality. Integral to this reality is the fact that everyone in the Latino community is both oppressed and oppressor. Caucasian Latinos have a hand in the oppression of Black and Amerindian peoples, male Latinos play a role in the oppression of women, most Latinos in the United States simply by living there are considered by many in the Third World to be the oppressors. Yet all Latinos by our experience of diaspora in the United States are oppressed by a society that continually silences us and renders us other. By no means do I equate all experiences of oppression, but "unless liturgical preaching can mobilize the needs and areas of marginality in those who are usually considered to be the oppressors, these will never respond in turn to those who are usually considered oppressed" (James Empereur and Christopher Kiesling, *The Liturgy That Does Justice* [Wilmington: Michael Glazier, 1990], 12).

PREACHING AS THE EVENT OF NAMING
LA GRACIA AND EXPOSING *LA DESGRACIA*

The Latino community locates its hopeful anticipation in the Reign of God. We are a people convinced that the Reign of God can and will be built. We cannot and will not doubt it. Thus, Latino preaching is hope-filled preaching. It is grounded on the hope that flows from the paschal event and the conviction that the Reign of God is at hand. The primary concern for the preacher in the Latino community is to call attention to the Reign of God, to uncover its hidden presence and to expose its apparent absence. In other words, preaching in the Latino community names *la gracia* (the grace) and denounces *la desgracia* (this word is used to mean "the tragedy" but its literal translation is "the lack of grace," which is indeed a tragedy).

Mary Catherine Hilkert contends that to preach is to "name the grace" in the community. This understanding of preaching presupposes a theology of revelation that locates grace in the depth of human experience, confirming that God's self-communication is found in human existence. She critiques theologies of preaching based on the Protestant theological perspective that "emphasizes the transcendence of God's word and the radical effect of sin on the human condition" (Hilkert, "Naming Grace," 434). Such theologies of preaching, she argues, have perpetuated an irreconcilable split between the sacred and profane. Its outcome is a God who is totally other and removed from human experience because humanity is too

sinful to come to an understanding of God's word. Ultimately, the
Bible is approached as the final word of revelation. In so doing, this
theology absolutizes the experience of faith of the early Christian
communities found in the New Testament.

Hilkert also critiques the pre–Vatican II Catholic concept of
preaching as teaching Christian doctrine. She attacks this view by
appealing to the basic Scholastic concept of grace building on nature
as well as Karl Rahner's concept that "human beings always stand
within the call of grace"; that God's self-communication is found in
human existence (439). The result, for Hilkert, is a theology of
proclamation that is grounded in human experience and a theology
of revelation that sees the scriptures as "a story-in-the-making—the
development of the tradition" (447). In other words, and without
questioning the authority of the canon, revelation does not end with
the Book of Revelation. The narrative of salvation is thus a dynamic
reality that is expressed in the concreteness of history and culture.
In this Latino theology of preaching, I contend that the preaching
event is the handing on of the tradition by telling the story of salvation. Yet if the story is not told from the context of our own experience, then the tradition is incomplete and preaching becomes a
desgracia, another dangerous memory of being rendered silent. To
fail to name *la gracia* that is veiled in our history or not to expose *la
desgracia* of the diaspora experience of Latinos is to fail to see God
revealed concretely in the life of our community and by contrast in
the experience of otherness.

AN ECCLESIOLOGY OF INCLUSION

More than a decade ago, the *National Pastoral Plan for Hispanic Ministry* (NPP) called for a new church that authenticated community
"open to the diversity of cultures" (17). It admonished those in leadership to facilitate the full "integration and participation" of the
Latino people "in the life of our church and in the building of the
Kingdom of God" (10). The ecclesiology articulated by the Latino
community in the NPP is grounded on the principles of communion
and participation. Communion is "essential for effectiveness and
credibility of the faith community, whose life is to profess and bear
witness, announce and denounce, and establish love and justice

among human beings in the framework of truth and freedom" (Marcello Azevedo, *Basic Ecclesial Communities* [Washington: Georgetown University Press, 1987], 194). Participation is the commitment of every baptized Christian "to build and serve the community . . . and to construct a society that dovetails with the postulates of faith" (Azevedo, 194).

This understanding of communion and participation in the life and mission of the church is the cornerstone of the ecclesiology of the Latino community. The use, the abuse and the absolutization of power are important issues in this ecclesiology. Such ecclesiology rejects the absolutization of power by any group, be it the ordained, the religious or elite lay ministers. This understanding of church contends that the power of Christ resides not in an elite group, but in the *koinonia* (communion) of the baptized, the community that continues Christ's mission in its unique and contemporary historical context. Each member of the community is called by the church to participate in its mission through the members' commitment to *diakonia* (service). The *diakonia* of the membership is called forth and determined by the church community after discerning the charisms of the Spirit that each baptized member of the community has received.

To view community and power in this fashion in no way threatens the hierarchical component of community. The project of the Latino community is far from being one that deconstructs the hierarchy. On the contrary, the hierarchy is integral to a Latino view of church and community. We greatly respect and hold dear the role of the hierarchy in its magisterial authority, and in the governance and pastoring of the church. What this Latino ecclesiology insists on is that the hierarchy be part of the community, that it exist within the community and for its sake as part of the community (Azevedo, 203). Again, the community is united by its common faith in Jesus Christ and by the mission of preaching and building the Reign of God. The mission is carried out in coordinated fashion through the varying ministries in the church. Some of the ministries are "fully called into being by the Spirit, others are associated with the laying on of hands and bound up with the institution and mission of the Twelve. . . . Thus we replace the linear scheme with one in which the community shows up as the all-embracing reality" (Yves Congar, *"Ministères et communion ecclésiale"* [Paris, 1971]; cited by Azevedo, 207).

The preacher, aware that community is an all-embracing reality
from which all else flows, calls forth a new order of relationship
within the church in which the laity participate fully and thus exercise their baptismal responsibility of building up the church community through their Spirit-given charisms. Because the experience
of being silenced and rendered other has no place in the church, the
preacher reminds the community that we are all equal in *koinonia*
and in our commitment to *diakonia*. The preacher should be careful
not to equate equality with the absence of differences in the community. There are differences, but they are meant to be used for the
building up of the community. There is richness in the differences,
for they enable a diversity of functions to be realized. Every member has a function in the community that is charismatically determined, but each function has the same goal: the building up of the
church community and the establishment of the Reign of God.

PREACHING AS *CONCIENTIZACIÓN*

Latino preaching, based on the principles of communion and participation, is committed to the process of *concientización* (raising consciousness). The word *concientizar* stands in contrast to the popular
term "to empower," which presupposes an ecclesiology in which an
elite group accumulates power and subsequently shares that power
with the powerless. *Concientización* is a process through which
people embrace their baptismal power and use it as an instrument of
their liberation. Through this process, the oppressed "discover the
causes of their oppression, organize themselves into movements,
and act in coordinated fashion" (Clodovis Boff and Leonardo Boff,
Introducing Liberation Theology [Maryknoll: Orbis, 1986], 5). Thus,
preachers in the Latino community do not empower people to participate because the members of the community, by their baptism,
already have the power. Instead of empowering, *nosotros concienti-
zamos* (we raise consciousness). To do so is to call forth the coordination of the many charisms present in the community to serve the
community.

Paternalism, which undermines the process of *concientización*, is
a possible pitfall in preaching the gospel of justice revealed in the
life of Jesus and its juxtaposition with life in the Latino diaspora. To

avoid paternalism, the preacher in the Latino community does not moralize in his or her preaching. The job of the preacher is not to tell others what to do, but rather to provoke the listener into a deeper reflection on their life with God. To do so is to allow the members of the community to draw their own conclusions and make connections of the Christian narrative to their own life and the life of the community. Thus the preacher in the Latino community struggles with the word of God and in his or her preaching openly unveils the struggle. The problems that our world and our communities face must be addressed by the preacher in clear and unambiguous terms, but "the rhetoric must be matched with thoughtful questioning and some agony of searching" (Empereur and Kiesling, 7). The paternalism that flows from simplistic, unreflective and moralizing preaching perpetuates oppression. The preacher must work hard to avoid using frivolous platitudes in his or her preaching because their use is insulting to the community of believers and renders the preaching meaningless and irrelevant.

Of great importance to *concientización* in the Latino community is the call through preaching to participation in the life of the church and its mission. This is done not only through rhetoric, but also through the symbols and metaphors of the community employed by the preacher. For example, the images, metaphors and symbols of popular religiosity are extremely useful to preachers in the Latino community. They are powerful images for Latinos because through popular religiosity, Latinos often express their deep relationship with God through art, music and popular customs (Jaime Vidal, "Popular Religion among the Hispanics in the General Area of the Archdiocese of Newark," *Presencia Nueva* [Newark: Archdiocese of Newark, 1988], 248). To use the images and symbols of popular religious expressions in preaching is not only an affirmation of the faith experience of the worshiping community, but is also and most importantly an integral source of revelation that the preacher must employ if he or she authentically names *la gracia* in the Latino community (see Orlando Espín, *The Faith of the People: Theological Reflections on Popular Catholicism* [Maryknoll: Orbis, 1997]).

The reason for the widespread prevalence of popular religiosity in the Latino community is complex, but it can be attributed to a high context/low content culture (Vidal). This is to say that what is said (content) is often secondary in importance to how something is said (context). This cultural dynamic has implications for the theology of preaching presented here. Jaime Vidal writes:

> [A] cerebral form of preaching, which relies primarily on the verbal element, will leave the Hispanic worshiper cold and unconvinced. Just as important as the content is the context. The preacher must learn to use his face, his arms, his whole body, to convey and reinforce the meaning of his verbal message: he must rediscover the arts of rhetoric, so discredited in current low context circles. Once again this is not to be done in a pretentious or overly theatrical way, but preachers from low context backgrounds must learn to feel comfortable and natural with forms of non-verbal communication which will at first seem to them artificial and embarrassing. (260)

To say that the Latino culture is high context/low content does not mean that what is said is unimportant. When the preacher in the Latino community preaches, however, he or she must be aware that the mystery of the faith "cannot be effectively communicated by merely verbal explanation; it needs to be expressed also in 'body language' " (260). For Latinos, the message of the preaching does not come merely from words but from the entire preaching event. Thus, the style or context of the preaching must be congruent with its content. When the context is incongruent with the content, the intended message is often missed or dismissed.

The process of *concientización* is one that is at the service of the community when its members embrace their Spirit-given power, critically judge their reality and act in coordinated fashion to build up the community. The preacher serving as instrument of the process of *concientización* must be one with the people, and must understand and share in their dreams, hopes and struggles. There is little room in Latino preaching for rhetoric that is disconnected from the reality of the people. To preach from the cultural context of the Latino community requires that the whole of our reality be addressed. To do so is to honor our response to the experience of diaspora, to build a just society and church where all are included and relate to each other as brothers and sisters as members of God's extended family.

LA FAMILIA AS ESCHATOLOGICAL METAPHOR

An appropriate preaching metaphor for the Reign of God as home and place of inclusiveness in the Latino community is *la familia* (the family). This is a multivalent image, not only because the Latino culture is family-oriented, but also because in the experience of diaspora, the family takes on even greater significance as locus of identity and cultural grounding. The Latino community understands family in a more ample fashion than the dominant culture of the United States. For example, in the Latino community, the distinctions between nuclear and extended family are blurred. But if a differentiation is to be made, then the nuclear family would include not only mother, father and children, as it would be defined in the context of the dominant culture. In the Latino context it would also include the *abuelos y abuelas* (grandparents). The extended family includes the nuclear family plus aunts, uncles, cousins, neighbors, close friends and *compadres*. The literal translation for *compadres* is co-parents, but the term is used to refer to the relationship and familial bond that exists between the godparents and the parents of a baptized child. For all practical purposes the *compadres* are members of the family. The word itself, which is not easily translatable, points to the broad and highly inclusive understanding of family that Latinos have embraced. Thus, this theology of preaching draws on the image of the extended family, one that is real and palpable to Latinos, and uses it as a metaphor for the Reign of God.

Using the extended family as a primary preaching metaphor, the preacher in the Latino community calls the church to authentic *koinonia*. Because the community is the all-embracing reality, the preacher does not impose his or her agenda on the community. Rather, the preacher embraces a bias for the community's common vision. In the preaching, the people are called to embrace and recommit themselves to the *diakonia* of community. Given that in the extended family the weakest and those in need are given the most concern, so also in the preaching in God's extended family. Latino preaching pays close attention to those who are on the margins of our own community and gives voice to their experience and marginality, thus facilitating the process of *concientización* through which they become authors of their own history and destiny.

Finally, aware of the experience of the poor, Latino preaching witnesses a sense of poverty in the preaching itself by being simple,
honest and faith-filled.

TOWARD A SPIRITUALITY OF INCLUSION

Latino preaching promotes a Christian praxis that is inclusive of all
the baptized. Gustavo Gutiérrez critiques spiritualities that have
been "geared to minorities" as being highly exclusive (Gutiérrez,
13). By "minorities" he means those in religious orders and congregations who were seen to live a higher "state of perfection." This
higher level of perfection was connected to the religious' separation
from the world and its everyday concerns. The other Christians
who lived "in the world" and faced life's daily challenges thus lived
a less perfect state of life. The spirituality of the Latino theology of
preaching I propose challenges a spirituality that is geared to these
religious minorities and opts for one that radically sees all the
baptized as brothers and sisters and fully participatory members of
God's extended family.

The spirituality that flows from the eschatological metaphor of
la familia is one that radically respects the baptismal dignity of all
members of the Christian community. In the Reign of God there is
no caste system with certain "states of life" that are closer to perfection than others. In the preaching of the Reign of God all are invited
to participate in its proclamation and edification. The casteless system that Jesus preached in word and deed must be presented today
in the same way. If preaching calls for an end to a spiritual caste
system in word, then in deed the pulpit needs to be opened up.

The preacher in the Latino community must be aware that he or
she is not the sole proprietor of the truth being revealed in the experience of the community. Great effort must be made to allow a
plurality of voices to be heard from the pulpit. Because the majority
of preachers in our community today are middle-class men, the
preacher must find creative ways to allow the voices of women and
the poor to be heard. To this end, the preacher in the Latino community, with the knowledge that others have part of the truth that he
or she is to proclaim, calls forth members of the community to form

part of a homily preparation team. In the reflection on the scriptural text and the text that is the community's life with God, the Spirit of Truth reveals the truth that is to be preached.

The homily preparation team meeting is also a venue where the preaching may be evaluated. The evaluation is important not just to assure the effectiveness of the delivery of the sermon, but also to assure that the preacher has properly named *la gracia* and exposed *la desgracia* in the community. The process of evaluation is also the best home for the community to verify that its experience has been adequately theologized by the preacher and that its unique story of salvation has been properly presented in the preaching event.

CONCLUSION

I end where I began: with the assembly as *locus theologicus* in a story from the Latino diaspora. Returning from my last trip to visit my family in Cuba, I was seized by the drama of a tearful goodbye at the airport in Havana. Standing before us in the queue for the final security checkpoint was a fifteen- or sixteen-year-old boy with his mother. I was moved by the love and the tenderness that she demonstrated as she caressed her son's tear-stained face and by the way he clung to her as if by doing so he could postpone the painful separation that was about to take place. When the time came to enter the checkpoint, the young man fruitlessly attempted to say his final goodbye but his grief had overwhelmed him. Gently drying his tears with her fingers and looking him straight in the eye, the boy's mother uttered the words: *"No te preocupes, mi hijo, Dios va contigo"* (Don't worry, my son, God goes with you).

These faith-filled words, which the mother hoped would comfort her son as he faced life's challenges without her guidance and support in a distant land, are words that proclaim the faith of the Latino community: God is indeed with us on our life's journey. To preach from the context of the Latino experience of diaspora is to assert the evangelical truth that God is with us and revealed in the life of the community. And to point to God's presence among us is the very stuff of preaching.

Rosa María Icaza, CCVI

Living and Sharing the Word among Hispanics

*Preaching to Hispanic congregations
calls for a deep integration of faith,
culture and daily life.*

A few years ago I was leading a workshop at one of our local parishes among faithful and dedicated catechists, when I was startled by a remark from one of them. "On Sundays, I usually come to our parish for the celebration of the eucharist and to hand in my envelope; then I go to [a non-Catholic church] to hear the word of God." What are she, a Hispanic woman, and many others looking for in Sunday homilies?

THE WORD AND LIFE

A few months ago, after I was asked to write this article, I consulted several people, particularly Hispanic, asking them what they expected to hear in the Sunday homily. It has been an interesting process. In many instances, the people responded in their own words with the same ideas proposed in church documents: "Help to live the word of God," "Application of the word of God to our daily living," "Some examples or stories of how today's gospel is being lived out by common folk."

Indeed, we read in *Lumen Gentium* (25): "Among the principal duties of bishops [priests, deacons], the preaching of the gospel

27

occupies an eminent place. For [they] are preachers of the faith who lead new disciples to Christ . . . By the light of the Holy Spirit, they make that faith clear, bringing forth from the treasury of revelation new things and old, making faith bear fruit and vigilantly warding off any errors which threaten their flock." Priests, bishops and deacons "must not present God's Word in a general and abstract fashion only, but [they] must apply the perennial truth of the gospel to the concrete circumstances of life" (*Decree on the Ministry and Life of Priests*, 4). In this way, the people can be rooted in faith and live their Christian calling in hope and charity.

THE WORD AND WITNESS

Jesus sent all his disciples to proclaim the Good News so that all peoples may become his followers. "Faith depends on hearing and hearing on the word of Christ" (Romans 10:17); however, this proclamation in words must be backed by a living out of what is proclaimed. Virgilio Elizondo states: "Jesus' followers knew their task was to go out to the world and proclaim what they had experienced" (*Christianity and Culture* [San Antonio: Mexican American Cultural Center, 1983], 29). It is impossible to share what we do not have. People in the liturgical assembly sense the emptiness of beautiful and eloquent statements that are not affirmed by a witness of a true Christian life.

As I asked people again and again, "What do you expect from the Sunday homily?" many of them answered: "a witness of the truth," "a compelling example of what it means to follow Christ," "words and example that help us to fall in love with the person of Jesus." Indeed, conversion to Christ comes about through love, not primarily through intellectual conviction.

THE WORD AND CONVERSION

It has been said that the turning point in our life may come through the heart, the intellect and the witness of action. I believe all three are necessary, since we are intelligent beings and "actions speak louder than words"; yet to fall in love we need personal contact and to experience the other who attracts us in a special way. There is a maxim, "I love, therefore I seek to know and understand."

In Spanish there are two verbs that translate the English verb "to know:" *saber* and *conocer*. We may know *(saber)* many interesting and wonderful things about Jesus which will lead us to admire and marvel at his sayings, but we will not be drawn to follow his teachings and his way to the cross and resurrection. We need to know *(conocer)* Jesus as a person who loves, understands and pardons us. Jesus' mission was to proclaim the Good News (Luke 4:18–19), to let us experience his Father's love and mercy, not only through his teachings in direct statements, parables and commands, but also through his actions of mercy and compassion, as he challenged the Pharisees: "if you do not believe me, believe the works [that I do]" (John 10:38).

Thus, the *Dogmatic Constitution on Divine Revelation* (25) forcefully calls those who preach to follow their words with their own attitudes and actions "lest any of the preachers become an empty preacher of the word of God outwardly, who is not a listener to it inwardly." The apostles themselves gave to us the basis for preaching: "We have seen it [the word of life] and testify to it and proclaim to you. . . . What we have seen and heard we proclaim now to you" (1 John 1:2, 3). Peter answers before the Sanhedrin: "It is impossible for us not to speak about what we have seen and heard" (Acts 4:20). Therefore, convincing proclamation of the word is based on the personal experience of Jesus on the part of the preacher and of the faithful.

THE WORD AND TEACHING

In the sixteenth and seventeenth centuries, catechesis was carried out through preaching. In fact, what we study today as catechisms from that period were really sermons. It was only with the invention of the printing press that reading and, later on, writing began to be common. Most classic and early literature, as well as the Christian faith, was handed down and learned by memory and repetition. Even today, at the threshold of the third millennium, many people in many places of the world are illiterate and rely on preaching and example to know Jesus personally. Someone has said, "Perhaps the only Bible these people will ever read is you." Therefore, preachers should never forget the teaching character of their homilies and reflections witnessed through their own words and lives.

Hispanic people, like many others, expect that if they pay attention to the homily, they will better understand the scriptural texts that have been read. We are looking for practical applications to our contemporary situations, not only locally but also nationally and worldwide. *The Pastoral Constitution on the Church in the Modern World* (62) expresses this idea when it invites theologians "to seek continually for more suitable ways of communicating doctrine to the people of our times." The homily should be simple in its presentation and profound in its content.

It is a good practice to include in the homily some references to documents that have been published by the Holy See and by the National Conference of Catholic Bishops in the United States. Those documents are written not only for the clergy, but for the whole church. Many lay people as well as religious men and women do not often hear about them. These documents make specific references to scripture and to the contemporary concerns of the world today. This also helps the assembly become acquainted with the issues that challenge our church leadership! Invite the assembly to reflect on and discuss current teachings among their families and their neighbors. In this way, sacred scripture and the teachings of the church will give the directives for their daily lives.

Homilists need to be acquainted with the social teachings of the church, with the pastoral letter and other documents about the Hispanics in the United States. Pope John Paul's post-synodal apostolic exhortation, *The Church in America* (Washington: United States Catholic Conference, 1999), is a must for all Catholics on this continent. The ideas and directives in it should be woven into homilists' reflections on Sunday scriptural readings. This is the contemporary teaching of the church, together with the *Catechism of the Catholic Church* (Liguori, MO: Liguori Publications, 1997). Those sharing their reflections on biblical texts can also express the insights they have received in reading and reflecting on the church's teachings, particularly those that touch the realities of their community and of the assembly.

THE WORD AND MESSAGE

Another point that Hispanics, as well as other faithful, look for in the Sunday homily is to see the relationships between or among the readings of that day. It is true that on some Sundays this connection is evident and easy to glean. Most of the time the first reading and the gospel speak of the same theme, while the second reading stands on its own. This is not a bad thing, but the homilist can help the congregation by reiterating the main teaching of the day as repeated in two of the readings as well as another theme that could be more meaningful within the context of some of the parishioners.

Perhaps the people have read all three readings before Mass and think that they are not doing it right because they cannot connect all three passages. The homilist will put them at ease and keep them focused on one of the main teachings of that Sunday's readings. In this way, the members of the assembly will be able to remember through the week one Sunday message in order to live it more fully. It would be helpful to the homilists to look at the verb in English and Spanish: to "remember" is to bring back to your mind something in the past, while *"recordar"* is to bring back to your heart *(cor, cordis)* what you have heard and experienced. Are you, as a homilist, addressing only the minds or also the hearts of your listeners?

THE WORD AND SPIRITUAL DIRECTION

For many Christians the only spiritual direction or formation they receive is through the Sunday homilies. Spiritual companions listen to three stories: the unique and personal story of the person, the story of the cultural group to which the person belongs, and the stories of scripture and Christian tradition. Similarly, homilists must listen to and publicly relate the scriptural readings, the social and political events of the world and of the community, and the cultural traditions of the members of the assembly.

Yes, homilists need to be aware also of the cultural spirituality of the members of the assembly. What are their ideas of God, of Jesus, of Mary, of the saints? Are they free to express their faith in concrete, tangible ways? Are they accustomed to using symbols that go beyond the material expression into the real meaning of them? Are they much influenced by the Hellenistic separation of soul and body, or do they consider spiritual and religious realities as an integral part of life? What is their view of happiness and joy, of life and afterlife, of sin and human failure?

Certainly, spiritualities vary from person to person, but given that we are born within a culture, we receive certain beliefs and attitudes that remain with each of us in the core of our being. In personal and spiritual direction or accompaniment, we ask, where is God in your life? How do you relate to Jesus? Does Mary have a special place in your life? How do you discover God's action in your life and environment? How are you responding to God's inspirations and calls?

THE WORD AND HISPANIC SPIRITUALITY

Among Hispanics there are also many differences according to their own heritage whether Mexican American, Mexican, Argentinean, Colombian, Puerto Rican, and so forth. There are also differences among persons and communities within these various groups. Therefore, homilists in the United States need to be aware of the cultural composition of the assembly. This might seem an almost impossible task; however, among those of us under the Hispanic umbrella, there are certain common cultural characteristics to our approach to religion and spiritual life, since the Christian evangelization of Latin America is the fruit of sixteenth- and seventeenth-century Mediterranean Catholicism.

God is all-powerful, all-seeing, all-just, but God is close to us and an integral part of life. God is not far away and many Hispanics (among others) consider sickness, death, failure and misfortune as punishment for bad behavior. However, God is also all-loving and the giver of every good. We honor God in the trinitarian mystery as Divine Providence. We hope to enjoy seeing and being with God in heaven. This is the God with whom Hispanics relate, not a faraway and impersonal God.

Jesus. Hispanics take seriously the Incarnation and relate to Jesus as to another human being: They caress him and take care of him as a baby, accompany him in his sufferings, and understand when he is tired, sleepy and hungry. For this reason, Hispanics believe that Jesus listens, understands and is compassionate when they share with him in prayer their concerns, their sufferings and pains. Jesus is our Savior and Brother and walks with us on the way. Any gospel passage that speaks of Jesus as a human being, with strengths and weaknesses, is very meaningful to Hispanics.

Mary is our mother as well as Jesus' mother. Therefore, we consider her very important, just as our natural mother is. She understands, nourishes and cares for us. She intercedes for us with her Son and has the patience and kindness to hear us. In each country, Mary is honored under a different title, a different advocation. The homilist needs to be aware of this differences when speaking of Mary to a Hispanic congregation.

The saints are our brothers and sisters and the friends of Jesus; we could say they are his immediate family. The saints, including those members of our family who have died, and, we hope, are in heaven, can intercede for us as our older siblings. Preachers at a wake or funeral do not need to convince Hispanics of an afterlife but of the mercy of God.

Expressions of faith.   Since religion is an integral part of life, it is easily shared with others. Hispanics express their faith through gestures (for example, the double sign of the cross), objects (candles), words (*"Buenos días le dé Dios,"* that is, "May God grant you a good day") and actions (visiting the sick). In fact, Hispanics usually consider both the spiritual and corporal works of mercy as ways of expressing their faith. Homilists may easily encourage them to put both into practice.

Symbols.   Faith penetrates beyond what meets the eye. Even uneducated Hispanic persons know very well that a statue is not the object of their devotion, or, in the case of Jesus, of their adoration. This is the main difference between superstition and belief. When people think that the power is in the object, their faith stops in the object; this is superstition. When people see the object as a symbol of God, Jesus, Mary, the saints whom they address, this is faith in the persons represented; this is belief. This would be a good point to emphasize when preaching among Hispanics, since most of us have a deep faith but some of us place that faith in objects that may lead to superstition.

When preaching on gospel passages that speak of Jesus healing the sick, blind, physically disabled, and so forth, it would be very meaningful to refer to the *curanderos* (faith healers) and to the gift of healing. Good *curanderos* listen with patience to those coming for help, pray with them, show compassion and perhaps gently touch the sick part, *sobándola* (rubbing it), know the medicinal power of herbs and recommend their use in the form of tea or ointment. Abusive *curanderos* may do all of the above but then charge a large fee and, worse still, make threats if the fee is not paid at the time requested or promised.

In some way, Jesus was a faith healer, as we hear him saying to his Father before the resurrection of Lazarus: "Father, I thank you for hearing me" (John 11:41). More often, Jesus attributed the healing to the faith of the person asking for the favor: "Daughter, your faith has saved you, go in peace" (Luke 4:48); "O woman, great is your faith! Let it be done for you as you wish" (Matthew 15:28); "You may go, as you have believed, let it be done for you" (Matthew 8:13); "When Jesus saw their faith, he said to the paralytic, 'Child, your sins are forgiven. . . . Rise, pick up your mat and walk'" (Mark 2:5, 9b).

THE WORD AND CONTEXTUALIZATION

Likewise, the person who is proclaiming the word, like any public speaker, must be aware of the situation and living conditions of his or her audience. People who live in the country, close to nature, would be apt to understand the minute details of Jesus' parables when he speaks of the fields, the grains, the seeds and the birds of the air, while those who live in a city will need more explanation when meditating on these same parables.

Children use simple language, but their imaginations are active and they easily understand the symbolic meanings of certain comparisons if they have experienced similar things in their own life. Perhaps not many children living in urban areas have seen a real sheep. Yet they may have cuddled a teddy bear or a shaggy dog more than all the other toys or pets they have. When that particular one is missing, the child feels insecure and does not rest until finding it,

even though there may be many other toys and pets around the
house On hearing how the Good Shepherd searched for the lost
sheep and brought it back, it is not difficult to experience the joy and
tenderness of that passage when we remember the time we found
something very precious to us.

THE WORD AND DAILY EVENTS

God speaks to all people and the ministry of the preacher is to help
all the members of the assembly to listen to and understand that
word. Homilies should really center on and elaborate the scriptural
readings just proclaimed. Perhaps some background may be needed
to place the teaching within its context, particularly if that context is
not similar to our daily life experience.

The Constitution on the Sacred Liturgy, *Sacrosanctum Concilium*
(35) specifies clearly: "The sermon should draw its content from
scriptural and liturgical sources. Its character should be that of a
proclamation of God's wonderful works in the history of salvation,
that is, the mystery of Christ, which is ever made present and active
within us." Given that God is present in our world and in our
personal life, is the preacher helping the people to discover that
God in ordinary events? To be present to God?

Many of the Hispanics who were asked what they expect to hear
in the Sunday homily responded that they wanted to learn how to
see God in local and world events and how to glean moral lessons
from them in the light of the scripture readings: "What is God teaching us through this joyful event?" or "What is the lesson we must
learn from this painful incident?" "We know that religion and faith
are integral parts of life. Help us to see that in the midst of suffering." "We know God loves us as Jesus reveals it in the gospel and in
his life; the Sunday homily should help us to affirm this in our hearts
as we live in a world of violence and death."

THE WORD AND LANGUAGE

Here in the United States, it is also important for the person giving
a homily or reflection on scriptural texts to know the languages used
by the members of the assembly. In some instances it is important to

offer a bilingual homily, particularly in Spanish and English, but this does not mean translating sentences, paragraphs or the entire homily from one language to another.

It requires good knowledge of both languages and a lot of preparation to be able to go from one language to another without losing the attention of monolinguals and without tiring bilinguals who hear the whole message repeated. It also requires knowing the cultural values of the two groups, since the message is heard differently by persons who value individual applications of the gospel message and those who place family and community first. The first ones need to be encouraged to share their personal and material gifts with the community; the others need to hear of the importance of developing personal skills and gifts in order to better serve the others.

Bilingual homilies are needed even in a mainly Hispanic assembly, since many of the young adults and children do not understand Spanish. Bishop Ricardo Ramírez, CSB, of Las Cruces, New Mexico, has a good article on this topic in the bilingual magazine *¡Gracias!* (January/February and March/April, 1999) written in Spanish. He gives practical suggestions in the second part of the article:

> 1. If the homily is short, it could be repeated.
>
> 2. A summary could be given at the end of the homily in the other language.
>
> 3. Consecutive interpretation without literal translation.
>
> 4. Simultaneous translation using portable earphones; however, those who have to use the earphones many times may feel like "second-class citizens."

Bishop Ramírez himself and other priests in San Antonio know how to use the third option very effectively. It is a great challenge but meets a real need that is going to increase in the years ahead.

If the homily is to be delivered within a bilingual and bicultural congregation, perhaps it needs to be a different homily for each group, particularly if the members of these language groups live in two different contexts. "The theological reflection has to be different, since God challenges and affirms each culture differently" (Eric

Law, *The Bush Was Blazing But Not Consumed* [St. Louis: Chalice Press, 1996], 124). As the homily is given in one language, the other language group could be asked to reread the scripture passages of the day and consider a question given to them for reflection instead of wondering what is being shared in a language not understood. Then the roles are reversed.

Another important point in the United States is to be aware of inclusive language. In English, masculine and feminine terms are identified with men and women, since almost everything else is neuter. In Spanish, masculine and feminine words are identified with a point of grammar since *all* things have grammatical gender; the neuter is reserved for abstract ideas such as *lo blanco* (whiteness). So for the sake of the sensitivity that we have in this country, those giving homilies should use inclusive language as much as possible. If the homily is given in English or bilingually, the homilist should avoid the use of the term *hombres* (men), as has been done in most of our liturgical books (for example, see the Spanish translation of the RCIA), and should be conscious of using examples and ideas that include both men and women. The homilist will be thus following the example of Saint Paul: "To the weak, I became weak, to win over the weak. I have become all things to all, to save at least some" (1 Corinthians 9:22).

THE WORD AND THE ASSEMBLY

Some homilists include their assembly by asking questions and allowing time for the hearers to think of their own life experiences. For example, the main message or messages of the readings could be repeated, then questions could be asked on how they were lived by each person the previous week. Think of a concrete instance and thank God for the revelation of God's love in that moment. This act of thanksgiving could be followed by a question about how God is speaking to each of us through these readings and through local and global events; the homilist could invite the hearers to rejoice in God's love for each one and for the community and to ask God's mercy for the present needs.

Finally, repeating the scriptural message, the homilist gives some inspirational ideas that would motivate the listeners to live out their faith in the following days, being more conscious of God's love and constant presence.

THE WORD AND STORYTELLING

Personal stories or concrete examples of persons living out their faith in particular circumstances are a good way to help the members of the assembly to remember the scriptural message for the coming week. Once in a while some humor could be used, but only if it is appropriate. Perhaps these stories will be retold by the faithful at family gatherings or among friends. Thus, the word of God will truly nourish their daily life.

Personal and other stories need to be short and to the point, bringing out the core message of the scriptural readings. The members of the assembly should be able to identify with some of the characters and circumstances in the story. It could be an example to be followed, since the hearers will be likely to find themselves in similar situations. If the story is remembered without linking it to the scriptural teaching, it is not an appropriate story for a homily.

THE WORD AND EVANGELIZATION

The theme of the Synod of Bishops for America (November 16–December 12, 1997) encapsulates the goal of evangelization and preaching: "Encounter with the Living Jesus Christ: the Way to Conversion, Communion and Solidarity."

Walter Brueggemann has written a very interesting article, "Preaching a Sub-version" (*Theology Today* 54 [July 1998]: 195–212). He points out that today, in our country, in our society, "God is still a cherished affirmation of *private* matters" (emphasis mine). This is not necessarily true within the Hispanic culture, since God is an integral part of life and expressions of faith are common in the way we speak. If you ask in Spanish "How are you?" (*¿Cómo estás?*), the natural answer even by non-religious persons is "Fine, thank God" (*Bien, gracias a Dios.*)

For this reason, preaching to a Hispanic assembly would be different, since we do not rely particularly on technological advances for the understanding and solution of our problems and concerns. In fact, it is difficult for a Hispanic person to say *"Te veo mañana"* ("I'll see you tomorrow") without adding *"si Dios quiere"* (God willing). Perhaps Hispanics would need to hear not about our dependence on God, since we know in theory and practice that everything comes from God, but that, trusting in God, we need to do our part.

A similar case would be preaching in a poor community. It is important to reflect on God's mercy and love that will never abandon the little ones, and less important to encourage them to share with our brothers and sisters the gifts they have received. Usually, the poor are more generous than those who have many possessions. So, the word of God always challenges us but in different ways.

It is precisely the preaching of a loving and understanding God that is what Brueggemann calls "sub-version" because in our U.S. society, violence, anger and hate are dominating the mass media, particularly television programs and movies. Preaching should encourage the faithful to be kind, just and other-oriented: "an antidote to a culture of violence."

All of us, but particularly new immigrants and poor people, need to hear of a God, of a Jesus, who accepts us as we are, who welcomes everyone without exception, who walks, feels and endures with us; a God who rejoices with us and for us encouraging us to lead a good life here on earth, and who is preparing a home for us in heaven; a God in whom we firmly believe, in whom we can trust and hope; a God whom we love because he has loved us first.

THE WORD AND THE CHALLENGE TO HOMILISTS

As has been previously stated, the persons proclaiming the good news need to back their words and comments with a life of prayer and action that witnesses their personal conviction and efforts to practice what they preach. This calls for a constant conversion.

Pope John Paul II tells us in his post-synodal exhortation *The Church in America* (26), "Conversion . . . fosters a new life, in which there is no separation between faith and works in our daily response to the universal call to holiness. . . . The gap between faith and life

must be bridged." This statement is very counter-cultural in the
United States, where the Hispanics' traditional value of considering faith an integral part of life is being lost. This value needs to be
affirmed and encouraged by the homilists' words and example.

In conclusion, we hear the cry of the People of God for homilies
that clarify the word of God and motivate us to live out our faith by
falling in love with the person of Jesus and to become in turn pro-
claimers, with joy and conviction, of what "we have heard and seen."

Kenneth G. Davis, OFM CONV

Cross-Cultural Preaching

*A poker game provides an
illuminating metaphor for the
challenges of preaching across
cultural boundaries.*

INTRODUCTION

Preaching is like poker. In both, one must accept the hand dealt. In poker, luck determines the first five cards received. In preaching, one also must accept five determinants.

First is the assembly. An ordained preacher does not choose his assembly. He is sent. Second is the lectionary. A Catholic preacher may not normally choose his own scriptural text; it is given in the lectionary. Third is the liturgical year. While a preacher may also note the civil calendar (for instance, the Fourth of July), it is the liturgy of the church that must mold his message. This leads to the fourth point, which is the context of Catholic preaching. Unlike the practice in some other churches, the usual context of our preaching is sacramental. Preaching is not the whole of our worship, but simply a part, albeit an important part. And the final card that the ordained preacher must accept is himself: He is male, usually white, and from a particular socio-economic class.

However, for this article I am considering a peculiar experience of preaching, that is, the cross-cultural homily. More specifically, I examine the experience of a non-native Spanish speaker who preaches in Spanish. He is dealt these same five cards and must accept them. Now as he fans them out, he finds that he does not

41

recognize them, is no longer sure of the rules, and most definitely cannot rely on a lifetime of mostly unconscious observation to help him understand the other people around the table.

He does not understand the assembly with an insider's acumen. Most likely, they are not themselves homogeneous. Rather, they are a gathering of first- and second-generation families who vary in their mastery of Spanish, differ by accent, and come from distinct Hispanic countries.

The lectionary texts sound odd and feel strange on his tongue. He risks public mistakes and consequent embarrassment. Competent and confident in his own language, he now feels inadequate and vulnerable, despite his professional education, former leadership, and past respect.

The liturgical calendar, which should be the sun-like center of his universe, now baffles him. How can Our Lady of Guadalupe take precedence over Advent? Why don't more people celebrate Easter?

His previously favorite moments, the sacraments, no longer fill him with the joy of knowing they offer God's grace. He now is filled with confusion, due to a profusion of apparently superfluous godparents, apocryphal saints and something that looks like an adolescent trial run at marriage.

All of this forces introspection, requires reassessment, implies culture shock. And yet he is not a missionary. He is in his home diocese, but he has not been prepared for how his nervous attempts to play the hand as dealt will affect him emotionally, spiritually and socially.

I've played this chancy kind of poker for almost fifteen years. After losing some of my pride and gaining a little experience, after bluffing through bad days and folding more often than I'd like to admit, I have learned a little about this gamble called cross-cultural preaching. I will consider each card and then make some suggestions on how to play the hand dealt to those of us who preach in Spanish not as a mother tongue, although at the cost of labor pains.

THE ASSEMBLY

The people gathered at a monolingual Spanish-language Mass in the United States include immigrants and others who, for convenience or preference, worship in the language of their ancestors. There may even be some who do not usually speak Spanish or understand it well. I know many young bilingual Hispanics who use Spanish only at church. They would never consider using it outside that setting, and yet they never feel quite comfortable praying in any other language. A former altar boy who has never mastered Spanish told his mother and me that despite his lack, he preferred Mass in Spanish because he "felt it in his heart." It was the language of his grandparents who taught him the rosary, the idiom of his parents when they were most desperate, the symbol system of the Divine, which, while mysterious, he still trusted.

How does one preach to a community that includes both those who cannot understand English and others who barely understand Spanish? How can one illuminate the experience of a poor refugee lately arrived and also an entrepreneur who economically has also recently "arrived"? One group has a practical knowledge of biblical metaphors revolving around agriculture, the other lives by the whir of technology. Their levels of education and acculturation differ as much as their command of the Spanish language. Their political, economic, and legal situations are diverse. By heritage, they come from many different countries that do not always share the same vocabulary. Even their devotions are distinct. A Mexican may not want a *Cristo Negro* (black Christ) in the church, but a Guatemalan reveres that same image from Esquipulas.

This assembly, however, shares one common experience: social dislocation. Hispanics in the United States are a minority almost everywhere. Indeed, even in those locales where they represent a majority, othat demographic domination does not often translate into economic or political power. The United States counties that border Mexico are both largely Latino and quite poor (P. Giovine, "Poverty along Border Greater," LATNN.com News: 17 February 1999).

Even the wealthy, educated, entrepreneurial Hispanic is often on the periphery. If she or he is the first college-educated person in the family, that distinction is a matter of pride, but also a demarcation from parents and siblings. A professional or successful business-person is also often the lone or token Latino in those associations and networks necessary to such success. Thus they may feel mar-ginal to both their professional peers and their own extended family.

Certainly a poor Hispanic is on the periphery of the "American dream." Teetering on the edge of the official poverty line, he or she knows that race, language or accent often prescribe where the family may live, the quality of schools their children may attend, even the public places where they may shop or play. Banking services, com-puters, universities, public-funded arts, all are often as inaccessible as Mount Everest.

Different authors have variously described this general state of social dislocation. One of the most influential Catholic theologians is Virgilio Elizondo. In his books *Galilean Journey* (Orbis, 1983) and *The Future is Mestizo* (Meyer-Stone, 1988), he explores the social dislocation and relocation of the Mexican American, and by exten-sion, other U.S. Hispanics.

Elizondo begins by describing the dislocation of these *mestizo* (mixed or blended) peoples in terms of two conquests. First, the Spanish subjugated the New World. They imposed an often violent biological, cultural and religious blending among themselves, the indigenous they dispossessed and the Africans they enslaved. New social categories resulted: The child of a Spaniard and an indigenous was *mestizo;* the offspring of an African and a Spaniard was *mulato.* Neither enjoyed the relative social status of the *criollo,* born in the New World of purely Spanish descent, or the ranking position of the *peninsular,* one born in Spain. The mixed-race people, along with Africans and indigenous, suffered the effects of that first conquest.

It was the *mestizo* who mainly populated that part of the conti-nental United States that formerly belonged to Spain, while the *mulato* were numerous in the Caribbean sphere that the United States dominated later. The United States was the agent of the second conquest. A result was the further social dislocation of both these oppressed groups.

Mexican Americans, for instance, are twice rejected. Mexicans may repudiate them as *agringados,* or those who have lost their Mexican heritage to foreign influences. However, those whom the

Mexicans consider foreigners also dismiss the Mexican Americans because they are too Mexican to be considered "real" Americans. The second conquest therefore resulted in a double social rejection or dislocation. They dwell somewhere on the space between "Mexican" and "American."

Elizondo then describes their social relocation through God's election of others who suffered a similar double rejection. He shows a correlation, based on social location, between contemporary Mexican Americans and the Galileans of Jesus' day.

Jesus the Galilean was also twice rejected. First, those at the religious center of his people (in Jerusalem) dismissed Galileans. Elizondo argues that vestiges of this bias pepper the synoptic gospels. "What good can come from Nazareth?" "Of course you were with him, even your accent gives you away!" Second, Jesus also suffered the persecution of the foreign conqueror, that is, the Romans. He must address imperial taxes and the deaths of those who opposed Roman rule. His own death was possible only through the active support of the conquerors.

Therefore, Elizondo argues, this correlation between the double social rejection experienced by Jesus and the Mexican Americans gives the latter a peculiar insight into the former. Likewise, by claiming the election of those who suffer rejection like Christ, *mestizos* can move beyond a world divided by supposed purity and resultant division to one of mutual respect and the consequent embrace of differences.

Finally, Elizondo presents Our Lady of Guadalupe as a model for all *mestizos*. She does not appear as a pureblooded *peninsular*, but rather as a brown Indian maiden, showing the *mestizos* how to work for a future of respect and unity in diversity. She chooses the indigenous Juan Diego, considered by the dominant culture only a passive recipient of evangelization, to carry the true good news to the Spanish bishop. She bridges both cultures. While speaking the language of the Aztecs and utilizing their symbols, she also blocks out the sun they erroneously worship and presents herself to them as the "mother of the true God." Mexicans (and now most U.S. Hispanics) venerate her because she entered their desolation, corrected the first evangelization and pointed to a new destination: unity in Christ.

Critics have called this correlation between Galileans and Mexican Americans exegetically naïve, even disingenuous. However, no one can challenge Elizondo's influence in presenting a powerful "semantic . . . sacred triad" (Robert Lassalle-Klein, "The Potential Contribution," *Journal of Hispanic/Latino Theology* 6/3 [February 1999]: 5–33) which influences not only other scholars but millions of average Hispanics who wrestle with their self-identity.

The question of identity, dislocation, and relocation in society is a unifying theme in an otherwise heterogeneous Hispanic assembly. Elizondo names it, analyzes its roots in the early conquests and resolves it through revelation. Finally, he provides a motivating metaphor in the story of Guadalupe. Although each Hispanic assembly is distinct and must be well-known by its preacher, this and other meaning-making metaphors will help the non-native preacher read that first card (the assembly) when dealt. The authority needed to preach to this assembly comes from the next card.

THE LECTIONARY

The draw that must be accepted and studied also includes the Bible as presented in the lectionary. Note the preeminence of the whole of scripture in this statement. The integrity of the lectionary must be respected, but equally important are the needs of the community and the scope of scripture. Thus, when the lectionary presents options, it is the needs of the community that should dictate which option is chosen. Also, when preparing a homily from the lectionary, it is permissible, indeed necessary, to look at the context in which a particular pericope appears. The lectionary text sometimes selects or edits scripture; it does not present all possible translations, variations or parallels. When preaching from the lectionary, one must consider the entire context from which a passage is harvested, well as the current context into which it will be sown.

This is obvious in the doctoral thesis of Pablo A. Jiménez (*The Use of the Bible in Hispanic Theology* [Columbia Theological Seminary, 1995]). Drawing on the work of Elizondo and Justo González, he suggests a hermeneutical principle for interpreting scripture in a Hispanic context. This four-step process presumes that there is some commonality of experience within Hispanic assemblies: that is, social dislocation, as noted above.

The first step is to "ponder the social situation of the Latino people." This must include examining specific congregational studies, such as Virgilio Elizondo's *San Fernando Cathedral* (with Timothy Matovina [Maryknoll: Orbis, 1998]), as well as such sweeping works as Justo González's *Historia del Cristianismo* (Miami: Unilit, 1994). The sociological studies of David Hayes-Bautista are as necessary as the interviews and case studies of Ada María Isasi-Díaz. All of this assumes that the preacher accompanies his people from a liberationist perspective that allows their experience to irrupt and inform his own. One accompanies the community concretely by living among them and working with them, but also by studying their situation through consulting the writings of those who have previously pondered that situation. Only in this way does the preacher have that "eureka" experience, a dawning insight that shows how the God of scripture is active in the lives and deaths of this particular community. From this personal experience and consultative analysis springs the *coraje y corazón* (passion and compassion) needed to preach a saving word.

The second step in this hermeneutics is "seeking for points of contact between the social location of the Latino people and the biblical narrative." The previous pondering will have identified themes such as those noted by Justo and Catherine González (in Arthur Van Seters, ed., *Preaching as a Social Act* [Nashville: Abingdon, 1988]): social status, segregation, status quo and false spiritualities. Now the preacher approaches the lectionary less as an uninformed outsider and more as a partner to the insider who approaches those texts with particular (even if unarticulated) questions and interests.

For instance, a concern for social status means one looks at a text and asks what it reveals about the race, culture, class, gender and education of the writer, the recipient and the explicit or implicit characters. This can make exciting reading, for example, of what is too often a boring rendition of the Matthean genealogy of Christ.

How would an interest in segregation influence the way we read the Old Testament's admonitions that the Chosen maintain their distance from the unclean? Israel sometimes sought to overthrow the status quo (as seen in the flight from Egypt), but at other times sought to preserve it (during the Davidic dynasty). How might today's survivors of conquest react to the conquest of Canaan? Or how may a corporate experience of injustice make a community particularly attuned to the prophets' condemnation of it?

False spiritualities claim that people need to resign themselves to fate: After all, God wills the world to have rich and poor. Did not Christ resign himself to this fact when he said the poor shall always be with us? Yet I know poor Latinos who interpret that same text as Jesus' admiration for the resiliency of the poor, the fact that they are not victims but survivors.

When the preacher thus changes his social location through this accompaniment of the people and an appreciation of the literature about them, he has new perspectives that allow him finally to see points of contact between scripture and the world never before perceived. Jiménez says that the third step is to move beyond recognition of simple points of contact to a correspondence of relationships.

Now the preacher is not looking simply at the text (although that is his starting point) or even to the narratives related there, but to the "correspondence . . . between the social relations that underlie and therefore shaped the biblical text and the social relations that underlie and shape our [Hispanic] experience." We begin to see that the Jewish experience of migration from Egypt influenced their relationship with God, each other and the world just as profoundly as the experience affects Latinos today. We see how power or its lack shaped the biblical understanding of God just as it shapes Hispanic images of God. We see how the question of losing a language and culture threatened diaspora Judaism just as it frightens today's Latinos.

And this brings us to the fourth and final step in this hermeneutics, that is, the metaphor or analogy that will poetically symbolize the dynamic "correspondence of relationship" between scripture and the experience of our Hispanic assembly. These may be such metaphors as exile, alienation, rejection and election, captivity or liberation. Some become analogies, such as *mestizaje*. And Our Lady of Guadalupe may have reached (at least among Mexicans) the status of archetype. As Jiménez shows, each of these heuristic conventions challenges prevailing myths, such as the New World Order.

González, Jiménez, Fernando Segovia and Aída Besancon Spencer are some pioneers of this hermeneutical principle. They are all worthwhile mentors when deciding how to play this second card (the lectionary). When preaching among Catholics, however, this card is always dealt along with the following.

THE CALENDAR

Only about 20% of the U.S. Hispanic Catholic community attends the eucharist weekly. Among the many reasons for this is the historical paucity of clergy. This does not, however, mean they do not celebrate their faith (Gary Riebe-Estrella, "Latino Religiosity or Latino Catholicism?" *Theology Today* 54/4 [January 1998]: 512–15).

Most Hispanic Catholic ceremonies have been and continue to be commemorated in the home or public square. Thus art, drama, dance and music have always been more important vehicles for preaching and evangelization than words spoken from a pulpit. The faith is presented in scapulars and rosaries, holy cards and home altars, medals, calendar art and murals. Plays such as the Christmas *pastorela* and earlier *autos*, dances like the *matachine* and public processions on Good Friday pass on the faith. Songs composed for the patronal feast and children's chants based on the catechism or the Sign of the Cross are still as common as the food typical to each season and place. Stories, proverbs and litanies carry the weight of evangelization in this still very oral culture.

It is the world of popular Catholicism, with faith expressions so ancient and revered that they are constitutive of this particular *popolo* or *pueblo*. Robert Wright gives a survey of the abundant literature on this subject in *Liturgical Ministry* 7 (Spring 1998). However, it is a companion article by Mark Francis that explains "the people's calendar."

Francis first looks at the evangelization of Latin America and concludes that it "filtered through the medieval popular religion of the Spaniards, [and] was relatively congenial to the cosmovision of the native people." Like Allan Figueroa Deck, he shows that the Spaniards themselves were still of a medieval mindset. Although the official evangelizers were educated religious, the majority of the

Spaniards who (at least by example) evangelized the natives were themselves steeped in the devotions and confraternities of their homeland.

Spanish laity therefore directly imported customs such as the *andas* or floats, and the system of *compadrazgo* (godfatherhood). Some of the friars, however, skillfully inculturated the new faith by "baptizing" native customs. One result is the beloved *posadas* celebration that commemorates the Holy Family's search for lodging.

However, these practices did not fall into a vacuum. They were "naturally influenced by their [native] pre-Columbian world view." Thus when the Chortís people of Guatemala were told that they were made in the image and likeness of God, they carved the famous Black Christ of Esquipulas—to the horror of the Spanish.

Since the beginning of the evangelization of the Americas, one has had to negotiate the devotions of the people and the liturgy of the clerics. Both follow their own rhythm or calendar. However, these cycles are not necessarily opposed. In fact, a liturgist who takes full advantage of both the flexibility of the liturgy and the richness of native cultures finds that each can be enriched by the other.

In the introduction, I mentioned Advent and Easter. Allow me to give examples of how one might negotiate between the people's devotion and the church's liturgy. For instance, Our Lady of Guadalupe falls on December 12, always the middle of Advent. How can a preacher reconcile these seemingly competing symbols?

Start by reminding the people of what *en cinta* (literally "belted") means. It is an idiomatic expression for pregnancy. Next, point out that Our Lady of Guadalupe is wearing a belt. She is pregnant! Like the church, she is preparing for the coming of Christ. This helps devotees of Our Lady of Guadalupe appreciate her significance for the Advent season. Now, however, one also needs to show the significance of this devotion for those of us more familiar with the Roman liturgy. Guadalupe also emphasizes the eschatological element of Advent. Just when it seemed that Divinity had abandoned the natives of Mexico, when their land was invaded, their people decimated by disease and warfare, their women raped and their children enslaved (all in the name of this new God of the Spaniards), Our Lady of Guadalupe appeared. The Aztecs were a very religious people: They had an experience of the Divine. Our Lady was like a second coming of Christ, an irruption through oppression, an adoption of what was rejected to be the elected. The native remnant preached the true gospel to the *conquistadores* who had committed genocide in the name of that gospel. The last were made first.

Thus the liturgy of Advent informs the devotion to Our Lady of Guadalupe, but that devotion also highlights the eschatology often forgotten in the tinsel and lights of crèche scenes. Both need to be part of our preaching.

Next we look at Lent and Easter. It would seem that Hispanics exaggerate the former and ignore the latter. Mark Francis shows that the Easter Vigil Mass celebrated with the people is a new phenomenon. It is long on verbal images (nine readings and the rites of initiation), but the drama is often omitted or minimized. The opposite is true with Hispanic lenten customs. The Way of the Cross is too large to fit in any church. It traces a bloody trail through the main streets of a town. Later the dead Christ is carried in procession, and finally the Virgin is accompanied in her sorrow throughout the night. Somatic, emphatic, tactile images overwhelm any word, especially if it is not sung. How to harmonize these distinct aspects of those celebrations?

First, take full advantage of the drama in the official liturgy. For instance, announce beforehand that holy water blessed at the Easter Vigil will be distributed to anyone who comes to the celebration with a container. I can testify that so many people will come that the celebrant will have to bless barrels of water! What a wonderful metaphor for preaching. People will take an image of baptism home with them; they will venerate it; they will use it to continually remind themselves of God's blessing.

Second, incorporate popular devotions into the liturgy. For the Easter celebration in Central America, for instance, women process from one end of town with a statue of Mary Magdalene and men process from the other with a statue of the Risen Christ. They meet in front of the church at dawn, and when they bow in greeting, the holy (bon)fire bursts into flame! There is nothing inconsistent with this tradition and the scriptures of the day. Rather it again gives the preacher powerful symbols to use in his homily.

In both of these instances the liturgy of the parish and the devotion of the people enrich each other. In both they provide the preacher with appropriate, inculturated, memorable images. As Francis concludes, "Time and again the popular religious customs that are part of celebrating . . . the liturgical year help give color and life to these celebrations." The same is true when playing the next card.

SACRAMENTS

While the majority of Catholic Hispanics do not attend Mass each week, other sacramental moments are of particular importance. Infant baptism is still very common. First communion celebrations are frequent. Funerals also bring people to church. Patronal feasts and occasions such as the *quinceañera* (a girl's fifteenth birthday) often include a Mass. Even non-Catholic Hispanics may attend Ash Wednesday and Palm Sunday Masses, especially if their own denomination does not offer equivalents.

When a priest or deacon preaches, therefore, it is still most often within a sacramental context. This preaching then must draw upon the symbolic imagination peculiar to the Catholic Hispanic experience.

The work of C. Gilbert Romero (*Hispanic Devotional Piety: Tracing the Biblical Roots* [Maryknoll: Orbis, 1991]) is particularly helpful. His use of reader-response criticism is an excellent way to bring greater specificity to the correspondence of relationships explained by Jiménez.

Reader-response criticism is partly a postmodern reaction to certain extremes of the historical-critical method. Absolute, objective interpretation of scripture is impossible. Even less ambitious hermeneutical methods are of limited use to the extent that they ignore the reader or hearer of the text. The preacher, while engaging the text, must always also be attuned to the possible responses that text will elicit from the hearer of that word.

Romero claims that the reader often must make assumptions about lacunae in the text. The tone or point of view of the author may be unclear. Characters' motivation may be obscure. Romero claims that Hispanic popular devotions are evidence that they have always practiced reader-response criticism. His book devotes chapters to Ash Wednesday, the *quinceañera*, home altars and penitential practices. For each devotional practice he provides symbolic analogues from scripture. His later work goes into greater detail concerning Marian devotions ("The Bible, Revelation, and Marian Devotion," *Marian Studies* 44 [1993]: 19–40).

Romero provides specificity to Jiménez as he points not to general themes (helpful as they are), but rather suggests how the popular sacramental imagination of the Hispanic Catholic interacts with scripture. However, I think an example both authors overlook is the folk drama of Hispanics. Not only is the felt need of the reader or hearer to interact with the text and elucidate its lacunae found in the art, literature and music of popular Hispanic cultures, but also found there is the peculiar Hispanic method of doing so. However, since scripture is written word meant for proclamation, the literature of drama (also written for performance) may prove most immediately applicable. Examples abound.

The *Auto del Niño Perdido* addresses the lacunae surrounding what the child Jesus did while he was lost those three days in Jerusalem. According to this play, he wandered the city experiencing premonitions of his passion. He sees a column covered with his blood, hears the cries of the condemning crowd and confronts the palace where he will be condemned. Only the poor have compassion on the lost, disoriented child. A rich man tries to confound his faith and tempt him with wine.

What poetic insight into the Hispanic soul! Popular narratives almost always portray the innocence of children, the solidarity of the poor and the oppression of the rich. They also show the power of fine rhetoric and the strength of juxtaposing symbols such as a tiny child and a cruel crowd. These are all opportunities for a preacher to learn from Hispanic reader response.

Another *Auto* explains how the Virgin Mary spent Holy Saturday. Anyone who knows the Hispanic family, and especially their reverence for motherhood, will be touched. The Virgin walks the street apparently suffering from amnesia after the horrors of Good Friday. She is looking for her son and asks each person she meets, "Have you seen the child of my depths?" No one has the heart to tell her the truth, and so she goes from one pious liar to another. Finally Saint John tells her the truth and she faints into his arms.

For the Latino, pain and death are community events. Compassion and harmony are valued even more than supposedly objective truth. This reader-response to the passion provides insights into preaching because it is based on Hispanic family dynamics, attitudes toward *susto* (fright) and the importance of solidarity in times of stress.

Legends provide similar insights. Why do the stories of the Three Kings always insist that Gaspar was Black? Perhaps for the same reason that legend holds that the three men who found *Nuestra Señora de la Caridad del Corbe* were each of a different race. Even during colonial periods of slavery and genocide, popular imagination, fueled by the faith, insisted that God's revelation is for all.

The *alabados* (religious hymns), proverbs and other snippets of popular wisdom corroborate Romero's thesis and provide immediate, striking examples of how average Hispanics have taken scripture (usually explained more through visual art and music than books or classes) and used it to understand how that same God is active in their daily lives. While the average Hispanic may not have written commentaries on lectionary texts, his or her culture has produced dramatic insights concerning lacunae in those same texts. The content and the methodology of this ancient drama need to be studied by those of us preaching in Spanish.

Today's *corridos* (folk ballads), the testimonies of charismatics or cursillos, the exegetical plays of Hispanic youth groups and the insights of base communities provide contemporary content and methodologies for exploring reader-response criticism of scripture from within Hispanic communities. These too bear further study. Thus while the following was addressed by Orlando Espín to theologians, it is equally true for preachers.

> The interpretation of the people's Catholicism advances . . .
> by delving into its *foundational epistemology* [emphasis in
> original]. Figuring *how* Latinos could historically and
> culturally think and image events, doctrines, or experi-
> ences has often proved more important than what might
> have been actually thought or imagined. (*The Faith of the
> People* [Maryknoll: Orbis, 1997])

I suggest that attention to Latino narratives found in contemporary and more ancient texts (poetry, song, plays, stories, proverbs, testimonies) is key both to understanding the Latino sacramental imagination and to discovering the preacher's own voice in an attempt to touch that same soul. Otherwise this preaching will never delight nor motivate. The people will be poorer, but so will the preacher.

THE PREACHER

This may actually be the first card dealt, although it is the final one considered. Justo González (in Christine M. Smith, ed., *Preaching Justice* [Cleveland: United Church Press, 1998]) considers the relationship between the social location of the preacher and the congregation in the context of the homily. While he primarily discusses his own social location, he touches upon the experiences of middle-class Euro-Americans. He explains that we often feel useless guilt and that this springs from an erroneous perception of our own power. He claims that in truth, Euro-Americans' "supposed power is gained at the expense of their accepting the present order of things, and thus becoming powerless to do much about the deepest injustices in our society."

Most priests who preach in Spanish in the United States are middle-class Euro-Americans. Most have probably never analyzed the power structures of our society, and when they do, most experience guilt. Thankfully, many are now given the opportunity to learn some Spanish and some are even given a rudimentary education about the cultures of Hispanics. However, very few are provided with any preparation or support when they experience the cultural shock of actually ministering in Spanish.

From where does this cultural shock come? First, it arises precisely from the realization of how poorly equipped priests are to do this ministry. Priests are taught, for example, to refer parishioners with chronic emotional or marital problems to appropriate professionals. That paradigm works for middle-class Euro-Americans, but it may not for Hispanic parishioners. What if the appropriate professionals do not speak Spanish or understand other cultures? What if the parishioner lacks insurance or even a visa? By default, priests often become the psychologist and family counselor, lawyer and employment agency, medical technician and notary. Priests were taught that Father Knows Best and later find out that Father Best knows how little he really understands.

The cultural shock arises from living, perhaps for the first time, in a neighborhood where the police are not perceived as friends of lost children, but threats to every adolescent; where schools are not considered windows to opportunities, but gauntlets to empty adulthoods; where the United States is seen not as the refuge of the storm-tossed, but its INS officers as Ahab hunting those same seas. It is like being raised in the innocent 1950s but graduating to the cynical 1990s.

The cultural shock arises from other Euro-American Catholics, the very people who supported us during the seminary, mirroring our own worst selves as they denounce the movement of "those people" into "our parish," even when that parish is rapidly being abandoned by those who built it and is now surrounded by others who need it.

And most often, this all arises in a parish which can barely pay the priest, much less any support staff, in a diocese only too happy to allow us to founder on the edge of ecclesial institutions, in a society where white men are viewed with suspicion.

As Euro-American priests, we preach to an assembly to which we will never fully belong, in a language we can never completely master, within an institution over which we have very little influence, amid the sharp edges of a still segregated country.

We do this alone. No school teaches us why, no association explains to us how, and no book explores who we are when we do what we do where we do it.

Who is this shocked, lonely, disoriented, stumbling minister? If he has wrestled with these issues, brought them to prayer and seen them in scripture, then he may be a very good preacher for a community that also often feels cultural shock, longs for community and is disoriented by the prejudice of our society and church. When we feel the social dislocation that our assembly feels, when we strive with scripture to discover with them a new orientation, then perhaps we dare preach about a God who elects what the world rejects.

We testify to the perspective this new social location gives us. Freed from the ideology of power and position we thought we possessed, we embrace the weakness that makes us strong. What was once seen as a problem is now perceived as a blessing. When we prepare to preach we reach not only to our bookshelf, but into our innards. Preaching will drag from those depths the memory of the teens we have buried, the marches we have trod, the despair of understanding another culture, the joy of discovering again how to be like a child learning to speak. We insert ourselves into the reality of our assembly, groan with the passion of that embrace, and mid-wife with them a word, a metaphor, an archetype that will articulate the torturous triumph that is our cross.

HOW TO PLAY THE HAND

I began by saying that preaching is like poker, but that cross-cultural preaching is like a poker game in which the cards are new, the rules have changed, and the other players are all unknown. But does that not describe every adventure?

I have found that I can depend on grace rather than luck. When the stakes are too high and my odds too low, grace assures me that no one is more generous than God. Every time I thought I encountered a problem that would not be solved, I instead discovered a blessing that could not be expected. Preaching cross-culturally has helped me to master three skills necessary to every good homily.

First, I have found that understanding the social dislocation Latinos live daily is essential to good preaching! The hyphenated identity or ambiguity of U.S. Hispanics is a theme of virtually all their contemporary literature and theology. Life is incongruous. Those of us who do not have the social resources to anesthetize themselves to this reality help those of us who do understand the real world. That is why the artful use of incongruity is essential to homiletic form. Suspended meaning is needed to sustain an anesthetized hearer's attention. Just as one does not tell the punch line to begin a joke nor initiate a murder mystery by revealing every detail, so one does not begin a homily by stating the major thesis.

The preacher, of course, needs to be aware of his major thesis because it must be the fulcrum of his entire homily. But he doesn't begin by stating it. He begins by creating cognitive dissonance, that is, by placing values vital to the hearer in apparent danger. Such unrest assures interest. As Elizondo has articulated this theologically, so the preacher must articulate this for the assembly. Everyone attuned to the incongruity of human existence experiences the need for a resolution of this inconsistency, incompatibility or ambiguity. The preacher counts on that felt need to maintain interest and ultimately provide motivation. The difference is that some of us have more social resources than Hispanics, and that we often use those resources to anesthetize our reaction to the incongruity inherent in the human situation. But disguising pain only postpones healing.

Incongruity forces us to re-examine cultural and social presuppositions, once more to reflect critically upon and to re-appropriate affectively the Christian story in the never-ending process we call conversion. But we cannot converse as long as we all smugly share the same assumptions. That is not conversation but shared rationalization. Any conversation with or about God must begin with a humble acceptance of the irony and ambiguity constitutive of the entire human situation.

Mestizos and *mulatos* live on the ambiguous cusp of human existence. That is why interacting with them can be so disquieting for those of us who hold to assumptions about who is "American" and how to be Catholic. I have found that living and loving with people who cannot disguise their uneasiness as facilely as I can make me more desirous of entering into a conversation with them that leads to my own conversion.

Since there is always a discrepancy between God and our experience of God, a preacher must always emphasize incongruity in order to open up enough space in our imagination to allow the Spirit freedom of action. A closed mind, a narrow understanding of reality, a rigid insistence on what we have always known and how we have always done it, stymies everyone. Even the spendthrift Spirit cannot enrich a miserly mind!

The second skill is analysis. It is a movement beyond admitting incongruity toward publicly and communally exploring it. What are the causes underlying the conflicting problem of evil? Why is there poverty in our land of plenty? How might we look at the unequal distribution of wealth? How do we move beyond middle-class guilt? Are we as powerful as we think?

Cross-cultural poker-preaching has taught me to suspect pat hands. Avoid simplistic answers! Look for nuance! Test insights! Keep on questioning the reality previously described as incongruous until a deeper relocation of the question occurs.

Analysis is the real nine-to-five job of the cross-cultural preacher. This kind of analysis, which discloses reality on a deeper level, is the fruit of committed, disciplined perseverance in prayer and study. It is based on careful observation and participation with the congregation. It requires a listening heart, a curious mind, humility of spirit and a habit of reflection primed by accompanying the other.

Analysis is the search for wisdom. And wisdom is reflection on experience. It is not content with a litany of ills taken from the headlines nor ideological reactions nor common sense answers nor prejudgments nor utopias. All of these make up the sandy foundation upon which are built all our cultural assumptions about reality and presumptions about ourselves. Incongruity has already disquieted us with the fact of our precarious ideological position: It is built on sand! Analysis discloses what could be or should be done about this flimsy foundation.

Elizondo identifies a key cause of incongruity among Hispanics, that is, social dislocation. He then analyzes the roots of this experience through an exploration of the two conquests of the Americas. Good preachers always do this. They begin by highlighting an aspect of the ambiguity that we usually anesthetize; then they analyze the cause of this ambiguity. Analysis opens options, explores new avenues and questions the why, what and how of all our cultural assumptions.

The final resolution will deflate the sermon and disappoint the congregation if it is not based on careful analysis that has been shared with the assembly. Analysis prepares for resolution. Through analysis we do not tell people the resolution, we begin to show it to them. This way the return to congruity is not explained to the assembly, but experienced by them in a way that they can then articulate for themselves.

The third skill is the use of revelation for resolution. If, through the artful introduction of incongruity (for example, the articulation

of *mestizaje*), we have disquieted people, and if we have led them
through various complications and evocations as we engaged them
in a depth-analysis of this felt dissonance, then they are desirous and
deserving of some resolution to their heightened sense of uncertainty.
Thus the resolution through revelation will not simply appeal to the
intellect, but will resonate with the whole person.

Christ used the most ordinary aspects of everyday life to provide
extraordinary insight into the life of God. "The Kingdom of God is
like . . ." He used metaphor or symbol, but not any pretentious or
fanciful comparisons that happened to strike his fancy. Nor did he
use second-hand, tired associations.

A lame symbol only identifies, it does not evoke. A good symbol
or metaphor is itself an encapsulated narrative event. It too causes one
first to recoil with a sense that the two things compared are incongruous, then it makes one reflect (or analyze) the possible points of
comparison, and finally one resolves the incongruity and accepts
that, yes, both the Jews and the Cubans have known a diaspora.

A good symbol resolves incongruity by showing that there is
continuity (through Christ) between the mundane story of our
banality and the sacred story of God's divinity. This is the power of
Elizondo's *mestizo* metaphor. It gives historical size and temporal
scope to revelation in a way that believers are able to grasp, although
imperfectly. As Jiménez points out, we can only participate in the
history of salvation through some points of contact between it and
our own "his story" and "her story." Symbol is a linguistic act of
faith in the incarnation: We can use examples drawn from humanity
to help us understand God's divinity.

That is precisely why a preacher must know his specific congregation. He must make these links using words and symbols that
they can understand. As God did not become some generic human,
so we cannot proclaim God to some generic congregation. We must
know their history, their culture, their nightmares and dreams.

CONCLUSION

Preaching is like poker. But one is normally invited into such a game.
To earn a place at the table full of Hispanics when the preacher is

not himself Latino requires more than just ordination. One must be willing to gamble what one holds most dear: One's language, culture and self-identity. One must be bilingual and bicultural. One must freely and joyfully accept this new social location, although the people to whom one preaches may never have had such a choice. Without God the odds are all against us. But betting on God is never really a gamble, although always an adventure. We simply have to accept that with God as the dealer, the winnings in this game are counted differently.

Three of a kind beats a pair because they bring more diversity to the table. Being flush with the Spirit is better that a full house of empty pews. And when the dealing is done, the winner is the one with the most hearts.

María Luisa Iglesias, SC

Participative Preaching: Laity as Co-Authors of the Homily

*Small groups such as RENEW offer
valuable opportunities for homilists
to learn from their communities the
concrete impact of the Word of God
on people's lives.*

A TRUE STORY

Father Smith tells of his difficulty preaching in his first Hispanic parish. The Sunday he arrived, the gospel concerned being like a little child in order to enter the Kingdom of Heaven. He had never liked this gospel because many of his childhood memories included playground bullies, cruel teasing and spiteful cliques. Whenever this gospel appeared in the lectionary, he would preach from one of the other texts.

Later, Father Smith joined a small Christian community, a faith-sharing group. To his dismay one day this same gospel text was on the agenda for their sharing—with no other scriptures. He reverted to his own social location and old memories. However, Suyapa, a Honduras immigrant, gave him a homily for this passage that he never forgot.

Suyapa explained that her uncle had raped her when she was twelve. The family blamed her boyfriend, however, and cast her upon the streets of Tegucigalpa. While pregnant or even when the baby was small, she could beg enough to eat, and slept in door-ways. But when her child was a toddler it was too difficult to keep him still long enough to beg, and people had less pity on a robust infant. She said that first she sold her blood. Then she sold her hair. Finally she said, "I didn't have anything else to sell except my body." And she did.

Since she was childlike herself, she was popular. She earned enough to pay for a small room, and the landlady watched her little boy. But she knew everyone despised her. The pimp and her johns used her. The people on the street grimaced at her. Even her land-lady sniffed and avoided her. But she said, "Every day that I came home, my boy would run to the door and jump up and down, and greet me with 'Mommy, Mommy, Mommy.' Even though I was a prostitute, an outcast and a disgrace, he loved me just as I was. That is why Jesus says we have to be like little children to enter heaven. We have to love everyone the way my little boy loved me."

INTRODUCTION

Since Christianity moved out of the catacombs and into the basili-cas, the dynamics of preaching have changed very little. One person, usually recognized by mandate or education, spoke and everyone else listened. Even with technological advances such as radio and television, this dynamic has not essentially changed. The number of listeners increased, but if anything, so did their passivity. From their living rooms, they do not now even interact with fellow worshipers, but simply listen alone.

Of course, there have always been and continue to be exceptions. African Americans engage their preachers by calling out to them. Charismatics and others encourage testimony by the laity. How-ever, in general, preaching has been the product of a lone minister wrestling with the scriptures in the privacy of the rectory. The past can be included through commentaries and histories, but the present is often circumscribed by the very limited experience of that single preacher. Even if the homilist prepares by using ideas from the daily paper, this does not affect the delivery, only the preparation of the homily. And it is still dominated by one actor, namely, the preacher who chooses which newspaper to consult and which story to highlight. The dynamic of one actor speaking and all others listening remains virtually unaltered.

This presentation argues that the reemergence of small Christian communities of faith in the Catholic church has begun fundamentally to alter this dynamic. Moreover, this shift marks an essential change in the way we do Hispanic ministry among Catholics in this country, a shift that has shown remarkable success. After a brief discussion of the full participation of the laity as called for by the Second Vatican Council, this essay will explore the RENEW process as a practical tool of such participation and will offer a brief theological defense of the participative preaching encouraged in such small Christian communities. The conclusion includes testimonies from those who have actually participated in these communities, since the whole point is that their voices must be heard.

THE SECOND VATICAN COUNCIL

It has been almost thirty years since Vatican II expanded the role of the laity in the liturgy. Subsequent documents of import to Latinos (Medellin, *The National Pastoral Plan for Hispanic Ministry*) echo this call and attempt to inculturate it into the reality of our country. Parish life all over the continent now is different, and people search for new ways to understand it all. Key to this understanding is how lay "participation" is assessed. To "participate" requires a change in a person. She or he must move from observer to actor.

How have we enhanced the participation of the faithful in the liturgy since the Council? The emphasis seems to be on increasing the number of parishioners who pray out loud and actually sing the hymns joyfully, receive the eucharist under both species and engage in liturgical ministries such as those of the lector or cantor.

We have had some success here. However, if an integral component of liturgy is preaching, and if we want laity to fully participate in that liturgy, we need ask: "How do we involve the laity in our preaching?" Here we find less success. The laity continue to be mainly passive recipients of the product of one active speaker.

Although the homily is not simply didactic, an analogy might be found in good teaching. An effective teacher must attend to voice intonation, appropriate gestures, concomitant materials, and so forth, while always attending to the response of the students to the class by gauging their attention, peer interaction, questions, and so forth. All of this is necessary but insufficient. The real test is how much students learn, or how that teaching forms and informs the lives of the listeners.

If the meaning of the word "homily" is "shared word" or "conversation," then there must be dialogue or mutuality. Only this kind of preaching leads to truly active participation by the hearers of the word. Like teaching, preaching must always attend to the essentials of good communication. But it must also insist that preaching affect the listener and invite the hearer to respond, and that response should be a conversion motivated by this "conversation."

There needs to be a greater perceived relationship between the Sunday celebration of faith and the daily life of a Catholic Christian. And if the homily is essential to the liturgy, then the laity must participate in it as well. It is precisely here that small Christian communities enhance the liturgy and the liturgy enhances the faith community.

PARTICIPATIVE PREACHING AND RENEW

Many small Christian communities promote participation by the laity in the homily all over the United States. Some call them base communities or core groups. They have been the heart of most successful apostolic movements (for example, the Cursillo) and many evangelization programs such as Christ Renews His Parish, the Little Rock Scripture Study and SINE (*Sistema Integrada de la Nueva Evangelización*).

RENEW is the focus of this study. It is a process that was designed to make parishes a "community of small communities." Currently, over half a million U.S. Catholics are experiencing prayer and faith-sharing in more than fifty dioceses through this process. Since its first days in the archdiocese of Newark, more than four million

Catholics worldwide have experienced parish and personal spiritual renewal through this pastoral tool.

RENEW has designed a connection between the Sunday liturgy and the parish that is based on the U.S. bishops' 1982 pastoral on preaching, *Fulfilled in Your Hearing*. They do this by forming small groups of parishioners, ten to fifteen adults (or, with Hispanics, adults and children) who meet in their homes to pray and discuss their experience of Christ as found in the Sunday scripture. That scripture (along with the commentary and guiding questions provided) is central to the prayer and reflection.

In these groups, each person is an expert since each speaks only about her or his own experience of Christ. Each person is always the only expert on his or her own experience of God's love through Jesus. No one takes the role of theologian or teacher. Nonetheless, there are ways RENEW avoids privatization.

First, as a diocese-wide process, it has the full support of bishops, clergy and other leaders. Thus small Christian communities are not seen as parallel or opposed to the "real" church. Rather, they are seen as renewing the church through the creation of small communities that network with other parish communities and the local church.

Such small Christian communities are not new. The house churches of apostolic times were just such communities. In more recent times church sodalities, confraternities and apostolic movements have often operated as small communities. However, today these communities often lack accompaniment or coordination due to the shortage of professional leadership.

The unique feature of RENEW is that its process creates just this kind of coordination through the training of thousands of volunteers. This is a second way of avoiding privatization. First, the effort is diocese-wide. Second, while everyone and anyone can participate, leaders of the process are carefully chosen and trained. Thus, while there is great freedom during small group sessions, a leader keeps them focused and maintains a connection with the rest of the local church.

A third factor is the RENEW materials. Just as the leadership is chosen and trained, so the materials are also carefully crafted. They insure excellent commentaries on scripture, linkages to the Catholic faith and invitations to reflect and act upon that faith as expressed in scripture and experienced in the participants' lives.

These factors have helped the hierarchy trust the laity. They gather as equal experts around a kitchen table and each speaks from a personal though not private space about what God has done in their lives (see Thomas A. Kleissler, Margo A. LeBert and Mary C. McGuinness, *Small Christian Communities: A Vision of Hope for the 21st Century* [Paulist Press, 1997]).

Through the development of the small Christian communities made up mainly of laity, the local church acts on the documents of the Vatican Council, as well as fulfills the major goals of the documents of the local bishops' conferences. Among these are "Go and Make Disciples" (USCC, November 1992) and "The Hispanic Presence: Challenge and Commitment" (NCCB/USCC, 1983). Laity experience a call to holiness and intimate union with God. Through their baptism they are assured of God's continual presence in their life. Their journey is a story of salvation and God's manifestation. They are encouraged to invite family and friends to read the Bible regularly, especially in the context of small Christian communities. There with others they experience how to deepen their faith and how to live that faith daily. Since the documents of the Second Vatican Council are generally not as well known among Hispanics as among others, RENEW has been particularly important in calling them to full participation in the church.

A June 1999 survey by CARA (Center for Applied Research in the Apostolate) of RENEW 2000 found a powerful correlation between belonging to a small Christian community and greater participation in the liturgy. However, as successful as RENEW is among white Catholics in the United States, it is significantly more powerful among Hispanics. That community and Asian Americans are the most likely to participate in both the liturgy and lay ministry as a result of their experience of RENEW small communities.

Bernard J. Lee, SM, did an independent contemporary study of small Christian communities in the United States. The study found that RENEW was the way most people were introduced to small Christian communities, and that successful communities seem to incorporate strategies similar to RENEW. The participants in the study numbered 7,500, of whom 20% were Hispanic. The study found that small communities appear to be even more important to His-panic parishioners than to those in the other groups surveyed. They meet much more frequently than other such groups and more often in people's homes. This may explain why these groups are so much more important to the social life of Hispanics than for others. RENEW is recognized as the single largest influence on people's interest in small Christian communities.

THE PREACHER AND HISPANIC
SMALL CHRISTIAN COMMUNITIES

Obviously, small Christian communities are vital to Hispanic ministry. Equally obvious is the importance of such groups in bring-ing Hispanics to the sacraments and into ministry. This presentation suggests that a preacher's participation in such groups, especially if he himself is of a different ethnic or class background than his parishioners, will have equally impressive results on his homily.

Imagine a preacher who participates in such a small Christian community. He engages laborers who gather with others around a chipped kitchen table and listens to them explain how the word of God has impacted their lives and how they struggle to live this word daily. "Preaching" as a conversation or a sharing of faith has begun. Everyone in the small community speaks and is therefore a "preacher." And everyone is also a listener. The wise official preacher uses this participation in the Sunday homily to choose a theme or highlight from scripture, draws on illustrations or applications from the group, even borrows phrases or vocabulary. That celebrant knows that the homily will reach his community because it is drawn from the heart of that same community. This is the participative preaching which changes the entire dynamic of the homiletic act.

Hispanic Catholics have embraced small Christian communities in significant numbers throughout the United States because those communities have "humanized" Catholicism for them. Catholicism in our country struggled through persecution and rejection in both colonial times and the early years of the republic. In our attempt to be "good Americans" our cultural expression of Catholicism became structurally correct, bureaucratic, and too much like a civil religion. My own mother, when she came from Puerto Rico, attended worship for several weeks in an Episcopal church in Manhattan because it looked more Catholic to her than the Catholic parish a block away.

Hispanics are often confused by language or are marginalized by race or class. Immigrants and migrants among them are separated from their family and friends. In these hardships, small Christian communities provide a new family, or even a first experience of church for other Hispanics who never connected with the Catholic church even after years of living here in the United States. To preach effectively to a people living in the situation in which many Hispanics find themselves is not easy. A typical congregation will have a mixture of Hispanics from diverse countries and all at distinct points of acculturation. Some bring a history of suffering at the hands of their political "neighbors," just as deeply embedded as the struggle between the Serbs and the Albanians. What is unquestionable is that "among Hispanics, small church communities are becoming an important and useful vehicle for the new evangelization to which the Church is being called" (*Communion and Mission: A Guide for Bishops and Pastoral Leaders on Small Church Communities,* USCC/NCCB, March 1995).

The celebrant is at more of a loss if he is not himself Hispanic (most often the case) or if he is of a Hispanic background different from the majority of his parishioners. However, the preacher who shares in the struggle of his people through a small community and converses with them about their own salvation stories is able to affirm and comfort, as well as to challenge them to greater holiness and union with God. In addition, he grows from the examples of deeply lived faith that surround him, given that members of small Christian communities "are constructing a discipleship model of Catholic identity that takes character from a newfound relationship with the scriptures"(Bernard Lee, summary of Lilly Foundation study of small Christian communities in the United States, 1998).

Preaching that springs from an encounter between the people and pastor in a small community of faith is an example of what Rollo May calls nutritive power, that is, power used to feed others. This is one of the great gifts of such communities because it is the beginning of public testimony to the faith. Recall that RENEW endeavors to resist the privatization of religion by insisting on the connection between the church and the public plaza or daily life.

Such participative preaching requires the balancing of several elements. First, the preacher who participates in a small Christian community must do so as a steward of tradition, but not as an imposer of doctrine. He must prepare with the training of a pastor, but be careful not to interrupt the dynamic of the group. To avoid becoming the answer man who short-circuits dialogue, he should refrain from comment until last. Moreover, he must always publicly support the role of the group leader and the rules that govern a small group meeting (for example, everyone is an expert). This, of course, requires humility.

Second, the small community itself must find ways to balance intimacy with otherness. There must always be a core of experienced, committed persons with their leader. This gives stability and continuity to the group, ensuring a safe place where true conversation will flourish. However, there must always also be ways of recruiting and welcoming new members, persons with fresh and challenging ideas. RENEW ensures that a small community never becomes a clique or social enclave by its insistence on constant evangelization, welcoming and continuous training of leadership and mentoring of new participants. This is essential to the conversation necessary to participative preaching. Just as the preacher must allow the group to discern and articulate the faith, so the older, stabilizing element of that group must systematically welcome the stranger who will keep the conversation fresh. Given the demographics of Hispanics, special attention must always be given to recruiting and welcoming the young.

This participative preaching is similar to what John S. McClure calls "collaborative preaching." The homilist and the hearers converse with a given leader and with agreed-upon community rules to establish the topic of a homily and the practical applications of that same preaching. A truly collaborative preacher will represent the dynamic of that conversation with fidelity to the themes, logical development and images previously discussed with the small community. McClure identifies several benefits which certainly are true to the RENEW experience. The first benefit is that lay Biblical literacy increases. Second, laity learn what preaching is and how it is done. Third, the gap between the reality of the preacher and that of the congregants is bridged. Fourth, the preacher begins to appreciate the importance of social location.

Finally, preachers model a collaborative form of ministry that is then ritualized from the center of the community's liturgical life. When properly formed, parish liturgy committees could serve the function of a small Christian community that participates in preaching. In a Hispanic parish in New York's Lower East Side, such a liturgy committee meets regularly with their pastor using the next Sunday's readings as their scripture reflection. To most people's astonishment, they began conducting pre-Mass preparations, as well as unique entrance processions that helped focus the congregation on the theme of the Mass. People started coming early because these rituals united this ethnically diverse parish. The lay leaders, whose creativity helped the preacher deliver a message to a congregation that was much more attentive, led these pre-Mass preparations.

The credibility of the preacher plays a major role in the receptivity of the listener. The Hispanic Catholic community has a severe shortage of native preachers. It is not unusual for a Hispanic Catholic to attend a parish Mass to receive the eucharist and then attend a Hispanic Pentecostal church for an understandable sermon. There exists a deep hunger for the comfort of God's word. Often native preachers help because they not only speak the language well, but also understand the cultural idiom of the congregrants. Since in general we always sympathize most with people most like ourselves, a non-Hispanic, preaching to Hispanics, has a credibility gap he must address.

Another challenge is that of class distinctions. While there are exceptions, most Hispanics still live in poverty. How can people believe in a gospel message preached by someone who is not perceived as being in solidarity with their struggle for daily bread? Or who has apparently never listened to their story, since he never alludes to it in the homily. The power of solidarity lies behind all good community organizing. The preaching from the pulpits during the beginnings of the civil rights movement is an example.

Small Christian communities are works of solidarity especially when they are networked as a parish-wide or diocesan community of small communities. This bonding with something greater than themselves is what enables them to serve each other's needs. In the same way, the preacher who participates in this solidarity bonds these particular class and cultural insights gleaned from a very concrete struggle to live the gospel with his own proclamation of that word. Without in any way diminishing the role of tradition and the importance of drawing on the experience of past Christians, participative preachers also understand the words of Pope John Paul II, who commented on the use of scripture during his 1980 visit to Brazil: "Since its beginnings the church has continually meditated on these passages and messages, but it is aware that it has not yet plumbed their depths as it would like. In varying concrete situations it *rereads these texts* and scrutinizes the message they contain, in the desire of discovering *a new application for them*" (emphasis added).

Hispanic people hunger to hear the good news as reread through the lectionary and applied to their cultural and class realities. Preachers who rely only on their own interpretation of scripture or solely on the applications suggested in erudite commentaries are spoiling new wine with old skins. This is why the U.S. bishops' committee on Hispanic affairs stated: "Since Pentecost, the Spirit has guided the Church in each age so that it can credibly proclaim the Good News of Jesus Christ. In our time, and under the inspiration of the Spirit, a new ecclesial reality is emerging—that of the small church communities—through which we can see the creative grace of God at work. Small church communities are a source of great hope for the whole Church" (*Communion and Mission*).

There is no greater boost to the credibility of a preacher than to proclaim the inspiration, the creative grace and the hope he has experienced in the testimony of his own parishioners. Even if his delivery of the homily needs improvement, he is an effective preacher because the people see their story in God's story.

This participative preaching invites both celebrant and lay leaders, as well as ordinary parishioners, to reflect on the liturgical readings at home, and to write down images, suggestions or concrete examples from their world that evoke the message of those readings. These reflections are brought to the small Christian community and shared. From this a composite may be created as an aid for all the ministers who plan for that Mass or minister in it. Thus the music, intercessory prayers, decorations and suggestions for the homily are integrated. When this same small Christian community is given a voice in the important work of the preparation of the liturgy, the living faith of the community shines through to the parishioners who come to the Mass. The example of Christian living is, after all, the best preaching.

For instance, one such community planned the Mass on the Sunday of the gospel account that included Jesus' saying, "Render unto Caesar the things that are Caesar's and to God the things that are God's" (Matthew 22:21). At the end of the Mass they gave a coin to everyone leaving the church as a reminder of the homily, which was so well-prepared and enriched by the narrative of their own lives that many were moved to tears. That week there were triple the number of confessions and new people joined a small Christian community.

CONCLUSION: TESTIMONIES

Countless such testimonies are collected each year and many more added to the questionnaire sent out by the CARA research group. A sample of what Hispanics are saying about their experience in the small Christian communities is some of the best "good news" a preacher can ever proclaim.

"Getting together with fellow parishioners and talking about our faith and concerns, and praying with each other has been very satisfying."
New York

"To be able to meet and share with people who have come into my life and shared love, faith, caring and being together as part of our lives."
Florida

"The opportunity to get reconnected to God, myself, and others. I'd been away from the church for over thirty years."
Florida

"I received the joy of reconciliation with my son, from whom I had been estranged for over ten years. My small group prayed with me and helped us find peace."
California

And finally from one of our own church leaders: "I've said that we need more homilies that are well prepared and meet the needs of the people. . . . There is, furthermore, a need to link the liturgy with social commitment. We can't walk into Mass, into church, as if we were crossing over to an island, separated from life's reality. Rather, we need to bring the concerns of life to the Mass, and then go back into life having been nurtured and inspired at Mass, so that we can carry out the commitments that we made there." (Bishop Ricardo Ramirez, *The State of Hispanic Liturgy in the United States*, Fourth National Conference of the Institute of Hispanic Liturgy, quoted in RECURSO: August/September 1989).

In closing, affirmation needs to be given all those homilists who believe in their people and who faithfully live the word of God. I am grateful for their example and the care they give to the preparation of the liturgy. As they preside at the miracle of the Mass they are witnesses to the new priesthood of Jesus, the Good Shepherd. May they continue to feed the people of God! *¡Muchas gracias y que Dios te bendiga* (thank you very much and may God bless you)!

Jaime Lara

Visual Preaching: The Witness of Our Latin Eyes

For centuries the use of images and dramas to present the word made image has enhanced and enlivened Hispanic proclamation.

It is a well-worn adage that "A picture is worth a thousand words." But no one has yet found one picture that will adequately communicate the meaning of those same seven words. Word and image go hand in hand, and for those of us who stand in the Christian tradition, scripture and picture are necessarily complementary. The "Word became flesh" implies not only that it became audible, but that it also became visible. The Word became image. As we shall see, this has been especially the case in the Latino/Hispanic heritage.

If one were to take the title of this paper at face value, visual preaching would have to begin with the proclamation of the definitive act of God on behalf of humankind: the in-flesh-ment of the Son in visible form. The apostle Paul, in his letter to the Colossians (1:15), makes the bold statement that Christ is the *ikon* (image) of the unseen God, which is to say that Christ is himself the visual proclamation of God's salvific love for humanity. The Latin and Greek churches have stubbornly held to the theological position, enunciated during the centuries of controversy over religious images, that the Divine is depictable and image-able precisely because of the incarnation. Hence, like Christ himself who is the Word of God to humans, the image is also a form of proclamation announcing the Good News of a God-with-us who encounters us in our visual and aural experience. Believers, then, are both hearers and viewers of the Word who is encountered especially in the audio-visual event we call liturgy.

Our common misapprehension of much of Christian art holds that it is primarily didactic; that art in church, liturgical art, was and is meant to teach ideas or truths which could just as easily be expressed by abstract concepts. In spite of the much misunderstood statement of Gregory the Great, that images are the bible of the illiterate, the truth of the matter is somewhat different. The art of the early Christian period was commemorative, formative and celebrative. It acted as visual exegesis of biblical stories; not just their re-creation in paint, wood, stone or mosaic. Christian art has rarely reproduced the meager details of the scriptural story in an unmediated way. Rather, Christian art was itself a particular reading of that story, the artist's reading of the story, and it was a real hermeneutic. The visual environment for worship with its scripture-picture could hold together past, present and future meanings which were experienced here and now in the church's life and sacraments. While historical lessons may also have been taught, Christian art was not limited to the rendering of "long ago and far away." Art sought to be a kind of radiography, an X-ray into literal, allegorical, moral and anagogical meanings hidden within the depicted story. The church historian and bishop of Caesarea, Eusebius, could even go so far as to make the audacious statement that "the evidence of our eyes makes instruction through the ears unnecessary" (Margaret Miles, *Image as Insight: Visual Understanding in Western and Secular Culture* [Boston: Beacon Press, 1985]).

A MEDIEVAL MUSIC VIDEO

At different times and in different places Christians have preached with pictures. One example from the medieval church is the illustrated Exultet rolls of southern Italy. They were used for the liturgical proclamation of the Easter message of Christ's resurrection after

Exultet roll, southern Italy, early 12th century. Troia cathedral archives.

the blessing of the great candle. Unlike a scripture scroll which was meant to be unrolled and read horizontally, the text on an Exultet roll was meant to be read vertically while being unfurled upon an ambo or pulpit (see above). These rolls are illuminated with pictures that usually relate to what is being sung in exegetical fashion, but which are upside-down in relation to the written text (Thomas F. Kelly, *The Exultet in Southern Italy* [Oxford: Oxford University Press, 1996]). Therefore, the rolls were probably meant to be a sort of colorful filmstrip whose images would appear right-side-up to those standing near as the roll was unfurled over the front of the pulpit. Together with the melodious words of the deacon, and by the glow of the Easter candle and the many candles of the worshipers, the rhythmically appearing painted images would tell stories about creation, the Fall, the Exodus and salvation. Music (audio) and art (video) came together to preach the resurrection message.

ART AND WITNESS ON THE CUTTING EDGE

Another instance of visual preaching was meant for those condemned to capital punishment in the late Middle Ages. In Italy, between the fourteenth and seventeenth centuries, brotherhoods were organized to offer solace to condemned prisoners with a combination of exhortations not to despair, prayers in which the prisoner could participate, and small painted images on which he could gaze until the end. Known as *tavoluccie* or *tavolette,* these hand-held paddles were painted front and back with scenes of the Passion of Christ and a method of martyrdom, for instance, beheading or hanging, which the condemned would be about to undergo. On the night before the execution, the brothers would preach to the prisoner by recounting the exemplary life of the martyr. The next morning they would accompany him to the guillotine or gallows, holding one of the pictures before his eyes all the way, even to the moment of death. Solace, consolation and the assurance of resurrection of both the just and the unjust were thus proclaimed, not so much by an acoustic means as by an optical one (David Freedberg, *The Power of Images: Studies in the History and Theory of Response* [Chicago: University of Chicago, 1989]).

THE ATTRACTIVE ART OF CONVERSION

If "conversion" literally means "to turn around," it also means to turn around and see anew. It is no wonder then that visual preaching has been a favorite and proven method of communication to catechumens and neophytes.

Bishop Cyril of Jerusalem used to preach his mystagogical sermons to the recently baptized while seated in front of the Lord's tomb in the Anastasis Rotunda of the Holy Sepulcher complex. The neophytes gathered around him would be invited to gaze at the open door of the tomb. "You see this tomb?" the bishop would ask. "It was you who came forth from the tomb when you were baptized and came to life." Their eyes beheld the geographical *locus* of salvation, grounding it in an historical event in real time and human space, rather than the virtual reality of a mythological archetype outside of space and time.

This patristic means of testimony and instruction was repeated with variants by Saint Patrick in Ireland, who preached the mystery of the Trinity to the pagan Irish with a shamrock, and by the monastic missionaries to the Germanic peoples in the "Dark Ages" who gesticulated and appealed to the visual imagination in an effort to communicate the gospel in the unwritten languages of the North.

Other significant promoters of the art of visual preaching were Saint Francis of Assisi (d. 1226) and his followers. Stories abound about the saint, who was a deacon and *predicatore populare,* and who used his body as part of his message. Thomas of Celano recounts in his *Vita* II (Chapter 127) how Francis would pick up a stick from the ground and use it in his instructions, pretending to play it like a violin as he taught simple folk to sing the Lord's praises in the vernacular. His most famous "pretending" took place one Christmas midnight Mass when he enacted the sermon by creating the world's first Christmas *crèche* with live animals. Francis himself acted as midwife to an invisible Virgin Mary and "delivered" a real baby boy whom he placed in the manger. Street preaching by gesture, song, picture and theatrical performance became hallmarks of later Franciscan activity.

THE PREACHER AS IMAGINEER

One such street preacher with pictures and body language was the Franciscan Bernardine of Siena (d. 1444), who was active during the apocalyptic days of the Western Schism, when there were popes and antipopes, and when it seemed that such discord in the church was signaling the end of the world. Indeed, the Apocalypse of John was one of Bernardine's standard texts. But as urgent as his message of individual and ecclesial reform was, Bernardine was not above using visual humor in his preaching. When expounding on the text of Revelation 8:8 concerning the four trumpets, he would pucker his lips and "toot, toot, toot" on an imaginary horn while describing the cataclysmic events of the Last Days. Or while describing the horsemen of the Apocalypse, he would pretend to be galloping in a frenzy and use his invisible whip on a horse seen only in the religious imagination of his visual hearers. Or again, he would be preaching

St. Bernardine of Siena preaching in the Piazza del Campo. Painting by
Sano di Pietro, mid-15th century. Currently in the Duomo, Siena.

on a particular sin or vice, to which he would assign the characteristics of animal whose sounds he would create with woofs and snarls
and brays (Lina Bolzoni, "Teatralità e tecniche della memoria in
Bernardino da Siena," in AA.VV. *Il francescanesimo e il teatro medi-
evale. Atti del convegno nazionale di studi* [Castelfiorentino: Società
Storica della Valdelsa, 1984], 177–94).

Bernardine used nearby architecture or created artistic works
himself to illustrate his street preaching. While speaking on the four

angels of Revelation, he called the attention of his audience to the four angelic sculptures on the facade of the cathedral behind him and on the four gates of the city of Siena visible to his audience. His own artwork was seen when he spoke in the Piazza del Campo (see page 80). He created a placard with a sky-blue field against which he painted the monogram of the Holy Name of Jesus set within the golden rays of a sunburst. This solar Name shield grew to such universal popularity that it was widely used as a talisman to protect users from evil. Its most extensive use occurred in the New World where its solar symbolism fused with the ancient sun representations of the Maya, Aztecs and Inca. There it acted as a bridge between the old pagan religions and the new "Christ-sun" of Christianity (Jaime Lara, "The Sacramented Sun: Solar Eucharistic Devotion in Colonial Latin America," in *El Cuerpo de Cristo: The Hispanic Presence in the United States Catholic Church*, ed. P. Casarella and R. Gomez [Washington: Catholic University of America/Continuum, 1998]).

Bernardine's goal was always to prolong the effect of his preaching by impressing it on the memory. This prolonging effect of his *ars predicandi* (preaching art) was coordinated with the activities of public penitents and flagellants and the charitable deeds of religious confraternities, so that the message would continue to be heard and seen even after Bernardine had left the town. It seems that he and other mendicant preachers, such as the Dominican Vincent Ferrer in Spain, had great success with such theatricality, so much so that they would carry around portable stages and pulpits to erect in marketplaces and city squares for their evangelical entertainment (L. Bianchi, *Le prediche volgari dette nella piazza del Campo l'anno MCCCXXVII* [Siena, 1880-88]; P. Fages, *Histoire de Saint Vincent Ferrer*, 2 vols. [Paris: Picard & Fils, 1901]). No wonder then that the missionaries to the Americas would repeat the same methods centuries later.

PREACHING PICTURES AS SPIRITUAL CONQUEST

The initial evangelization of the New World was accomplished in part by images and metaphors. The sixteenth-century chronicles of eyewitnesses make clear that communication was a tremendous problem and concern for the missionary friars, the Franciscans,

Dominicans and Augustinians who were the first wave of the "spiritual conquest." For both native Americans and for Europeans, part of the job was to make sense of the other and to find sense in the other. Unfortunately, since the native Americans did not have a written discursive language (some had pictographs which represented objects and general ideas), we have little by which to judge their side of the conversation. From the missionaries' side, great effort was made to create dictionaries, grammars and encyclopedias of culture and religious beliefs. Missionaries were chosen in Europe for their ability to speak several languages and to learn several more. Early attempts at communication had been by hand and facial gestures, signs and mimicry, none of which were precise enough to communicate the gospel message. Columbus had pointed to the sky as the locale of the God who had sent him to the American shores, but one wonders how much was understood by the native population.

The conquistador Hernán Cortés, arriving in New Spain (Mexico) in 1519, had his chaplains "dialogue" on theology and the Trinity with the Aztec priests, but no one knows how much was lost in the translations which required three or more languages to get words into each other's idiom. Then there was the problem of the innumerable dialects and regional differences in terminology even for simple household items. Visual testimony, in many ways, had greater success.

Friar Pedro de Gante was the first Franciscan to arrive in New Spain in 1523 and the first to create a catechism entirely in ideographs. Using the pre-Columbian penchant for images, Friar Pedro ingeniously created visual equivalents for each of the phrases or ideas represented in the Our Father, the Creed, the Hail Mary, and so forth, often with great inventiveness and daring (see page 83). Catechisms, confession guides and prayer books soon appeared in ideograms. But it was Friar Jacobo de Testera who saw the need to preach in pictures sometime around 1529. He created what was to become standard equipment for missionary preachers for the next three centuries: a series of rolled animal hides on which various images could be quickly painted, portable "blackboards" for visualized rhetoric. One such unrolled preaching aid, on the Creation (page 84), appears in Friar Diego de Valadés *Rhetorica Christiana* (Perugia, 1579).

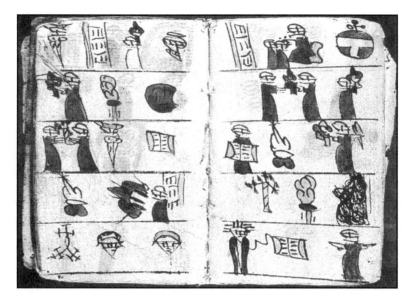

Ideographic catechism of Friar Pedro de Gante. Mexico, c. 1525. Currently in the Biblioteca Nacional de Madrid.

Sometimes the pictures were combined with a word or a simple phrase written in the native language (using the Roman alphabet), which would act to remind the preacher of his new theological vocabulary. In other instances, pictures were set up in church near the pulpit and the friar would preach using a pointer to indicate, as shown on page 87, the progression of Christ's passion and death (Juan Guillermo Duran, *Monumenta Catechetica Hispanoamericana* [Buenos Aires: Pontificia Universidad Católica Argentina, 1984]).

As with their spiritual forebears in Europe, outdoor preaching was common for the New World mendicants. Permanent as well as ephemeral pulpits were constructed outdoors for the weekly hour-long preaching that usually preceded the eucharistic celebration. Such pulpits or preaching balconies were often lined with colorful frescos depicting the same themes that Bernardine of Siena expounded— the End Times.

One of the most difficult concepts to communicate to the neo-phytes was that of personal responsibility for deeds and the result-ing reward or punishment in this world or the next. Pre-Columbian

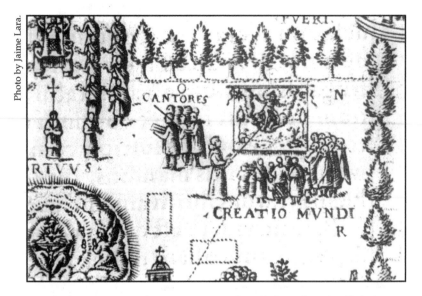

Detail of an engraving from Friar Diego de Valadés, *Rhetorica Christiana*, Perugia, 1579. Courtesy Franciscan Archives of America.

Americans did not have the notion of sin, in our theological sense of the word. The notion of transgressions of established behavior was familiar, although often thought to be the result of outside causality, either that of the gods or of fate, but personal responsibility and its consequences were unknown. Thus, the Christian missionaries had to find ways to demonstrate to the neophytes that their free choices and actions in themselves were either good or evil, and would have consequences in the hereafter. The most common way to demonstrate the Christian concept was with visual images of Christ's return, the Last Judgment, and the resulting rewards or punishment in heaven or hell. We find these outdoor fresco scenes in great quantity, often depicting sins considered common to the native peoples—such as idolatry, drunkenness and lust—and located where they would act as backdrops to reinforce the preaching. Thus art in the evangelization of the Americas was not merely decorative, but instructional and illustrative of the spoken word.

The success of this type of visual communication has not been lost on more modern missionaries. In the late nineteenth century, the

Church of Jesus Christ of the Latter-Day Saints commissioned an illustrated *Book of Mormon* consisting entirely of painted images to be mounted on scrolls or rollers as a continuous panorama for motivational instruction among indigenous peoples (*C.A. Christensen: Mormon Painter,* exhibition catalogue, Museum of Church History and Art, Salt Lake City, 1984).

THE THEATRICAL HOMILY

If art was one way in which the spoken word was made visible, then the theatrical arts gave an added dimension. Religious theater started at the inception of the evangelization of the New World. It appealed to the indigenous, who were accustomed to theatrical performances in their ancient religion and in their temples. A survey of sixteenth-century drama in Mexico shows that it had two thrusts: moral indoctrination and eschatological preparation. The conversion of the New World was thought to be the beginning of the end of the world—as prophesied in the Bible and in medieval theology and legends—and thus there was an urgency to convert, baptize and prepare for the End. Amerindians were exposed to and entertained by such dramas as the *Destruction of Jerusalem,* the *Reconquest of the Holy City,* the *Prophecies of Daniel,* the *Last Judgment* and similar presentations with extensive narration. We have evidence that the dramas were used in place of sermons, that is, they became the preaching itself. Some were "Hollywood" spectacles with a cast of native extras in the hundreds. Elaborate costumes and staging did more than entertain. The details of the performance convinced the audience of the reality and actuality of the sacred events—the evidence of their eyes—doing what good preaching had always done and what preachers like Bernardine of Siena had accomplished in their own way (José Rojas Garcidueñas, *Autos y Coloquios del Siglo XVI* [Mexico: Universidad Nacional Autónoma, 1939]). So intent on communicating with impact and force were the early missionaries that they did not refrain from using some now-questionable props in their visual sermons. When the Augustinians in Mexico preached on the horrors of eternal punishment that awaited the unrepentant, they created huge bonfires in front of their audience and threw in live dogs and cats! The howls and screams of the animal exemplars were said to have brought the desired tears of contrition to the new believers. Likewise, when the Jesuits—who prided themselves on being the new wave of Counter-Reformation preachers—staged the *Last Judgment* for Inca converts, they had their charges acquire props by exhuming bones and cadavers from the cemeteries for the discourse on the Resurrection of the Dead. Luckily for the recently dead and the local fauna, such extremes were rare (Fernando Horcasitas, *El Teatro Náhuatl: épocas novohispana y moderna* [Mexico: Universidad Nacional Autónoma, 1974]).

In addition, there were theatrical performances within liturgies and liturgical events within theatrical performances. Real sacramental baptisms took place during performances of the *Life of John the Baptist* and the *Conquest of Jerusalem*. In the latter, the infidel actors portraying Muslims were in reality native catechumens who, at the moment of "surrendering" the Holy City to the Christians, "accepted" baptism from the hands of a friar at the instruction of an Indian actor-pope. Meanwhile, the blessed sacrament of the eucharist was "watching" all of this from its own stage platform, because the play was only a pause during an extended Corpus Christi procession honoring the sacrament (Robert Ricard, *The Spiritual Conquest of Mexico* [Berkeley: University of California Press, 1966]).

Toward the end of the sixteenth century, a type of preaching theater was invented in Mexico, the *neixcuitilli* (examples). These were mute dramas enacted during the Sunday sermon. As the preacher was speaking, native thespians would silently act out his words, usually a story or episode from the scriptures with a moral lesson. These *neixcuitilli* were popular for at least a century. Thus, it is no exaggeration to say that the evangelization of America was due in large part to the success of a visual locution which was not entirely a monologue, but which allowed for some dialogue between Amerindian and European cultures and religious sensibilities.

The christianization of the American continent was also accomplished in large part by a change in metaphor. The root metaphor of ancient America had been tied largely to blood and sun. All the

Detail of an engraving from Friar Diego de Valadés, *Rhetorica Christiana*, Perugia, 1579. Courtesy Franciscan Archives of America.

peoples of the great Amerindian civilizations—Aztecs, Incas, Maya, Chibchas, Taino—seem to have practiced human sacrifice in some form and to have worshiped solar deities. The visual preaching of the missionaries, in the context of a new liturgy, music, sculpture, painting and architecture, allowed for a shift in that root metaphor to a new blood and a new sun—the Sun of Justice who shed redemptive blood on the cross once for all (Lara, 1998).

PERSONAL TESTIMONY IN PUBLIC PLACES

Our last example of visual preaching uses the word in an elastic sense—"preaching" here meaning testimony or witness before other's eyes about one's faith in God and God's providence. Certainly one example is the public procession. Outdoor processions have been the norm among Latin American Catholics since the first moment of the "spiritual conquest." All the pre-Columbian cultures of America had forms of civil religion that involved choreographed movement, dance or communal procession. It is no wonder then that Catholic liturgical events appealed so directly to the natives with their color, incense, pomp and pageantry. Indeed, the missionaries actively looked for ways to fuse the new religion onto the old without dilution. They sought to fill the ritual vacuum left by the extirpation of the idols and the destruction of the temples with new and grander constructions of churches, churchyards, wayside chapels, monumental outdoor crosses and murals. They also searched for dynamic equivalences of words, gestures, images and material objects that could give the new Christian sense of time, space and life, and simultaneously retain familiar practices, objects and patterns in a new light (Luis Balquiedra, "The Liturgical Principles Used by Missionaries and the Missionary Background to the Christianization of the Philippines," *Philippiniana Sacra* 30/88 [January-April 1995]: 5–79). Thus, they anticipated by four centuries the thought of the Second Vatican Council that "the Church considers with sympathy and, if possible, preserves intact the elements in these peoples' way of life that are not indissolubly bound up with superstition and error. Sometimes in fact the Church admits such elements into the liturgy itself, provided they are in keeping with the true and authentic spirit of the liturgy" (*Sacrosantum Concilium* 37).

Processions in Latin American society tend to be circular. That is, they end where they begin, being a sort of "pied piper" event that rounds up the faithful as the procession traverses the city or town. In the colonial period, and in many locales today, the procession starts in the church building and makes stops or stations at chapels or temporary altars constructed along the route. The movement as well as the pauses are accompanied by singing and the carrying of religious objects, such as the banner of the confraternity sponsoring the procession, statues or the eucharist. At an early date, dance was incorporated into the processions, just as it had been in pre-Columbian times. In Mexico, the *mitotes* or line dances continued in Christian religious ceremonies. In Colombia, it is evident that colonial Amerindians and Negroes had learned the medieval *tripudium* (three-step), in which the whole processional line takes three steps forward and two steps back, not unlike a religious *conga* line. This ancient dance symbolized spiritual progression and regression, and the gradual, snail-like advance of the sinner toward the heavenly goal.

The procession was also a public forum for the demonstration of faith and devotion. It was an arena where ardent faith could be stirred up in the spectators by the marchers, penitents and flagellants. It responded to the human need to externalize one's belief, so typical of Catholic Christianity and so foreign to sixteenth-century Reformation, Pietist and Quietist movements (Susan Verdi Webster, "The Descent from the Cross in Sixteenth-Century New Spain," *The Early Drama, Art, and Music Review* 19/2 [1997]: 69–85).

Another public testimony was accomplished by the objects we call *milagros* (miracles) and *retablos* (retables). *Milagros* are the votive offerings from the faithful that in Latin American Christianity festoon a statue or altar. Commonly these can be flowers, photographs, medals, handwritten notes, holy cards, rosaries, and tiny silver or gold images of body parts, animals, plants and domestic articles. They are offered to the holy personage in thanks for his or her intercession in response to a petitioner's prayers. They commemorate a "miracle"—a child cured of illness, a fruitful harvest, a soldier-son returned home, and so on. Because they are a type of votive offering, *milagros* are often referred to as *ex-votos*, meaning "from a vow." Like so many aspects of Latino Catholicism, they have similarities to customs and objects of pre-conquest culture wherein some tangible form of thanksgiving was made to the gods; those pagan forms were later joined to Catholic traditions. Body-part *milagros,* for example, have their origin in similar body-part reliquaries common in medieval Europe. The displayed part of the body was a symbol of the locus of the desired or received miracle. In Latin America, miniature silver eyes and feet seem to be the most commonly represented shapes because of the prevalence of blindness and lameness among the poor (Martha Egan, *Milagros: Votive Offering from the Americas* [Santa Fe: Museum of New Mexico Press, 1991]).

A related form of *ex-voto* are folk paintings on tin, wood, paper or canvas that depict the story of the miraculous cure or rescue and are called *retablos, láminas* or *santos sobre hojas de lata.* They have received the misnomer of *retablo* (retable), which originally referred to the decorative monumental panels placed behind the altar table

Retablo, early twentieth-century. Private collection.

in church. Unlike the *milagros*, they are essentially narrative in nature and are closer to our concept of preaching or witnessing through pictures. These tinplate testators reached their greatest popularity in the nineteenth century, and are today collectors' items, especially in the Southwest of the United States. The stories they tell are often quite moving and involve dramatic scenes of divine rescue from falling walls, speeding locomotives and stampeding horses (above). The recipient of the miracles would commission a folk artist to render the story in a direct and unsophisticated manner. The date, place and circumstances of the divine intervention would be painted onto the image, thus joining text and picture. The *retablo* would be displayed in a public place, usually on the interior wall of the parish church where it could inspire others to seek the help of the same saint.

According to Kenneth Davis, *retablos* are part of the remote history of such modern lay Catholic preaching as that done by charismatics or cursillistas. Both are personal, not private, testimony given in public, meant to inspire and instruct. Both are formulaic, petitionary and lay-based. The later oral testimony is an example of contemporary adaptation of earlier visual popular religious symbols.

Though small in size and made of an inexpensive material like tinplate, the *retablo* was a picture-scripture proclaiming the faith fact that God does indeed intervene on our behalf in human history (Gloria Fraser Giffords, *The Art of Private Devotion: Retablo Painting of Mexico* [Fort Worth: InterCultura and Meadows Museum, 1991]).

TECHNOLOGY AND PREACHING

At the cusp of this new millennium, we are more conscious than ever of the power of the visual image. Technology has brought us numerous means of communication by word and image, but it is the latter that seems to impact us most. It is of no little importance that computer technology and the Internet have restored the ancient word "icon" to the tongue of every computer-literate individual. Our visual vocabulary has made "clicking on icons" as common as "channel surfing."

Some ecclesial groups have experimented with visual preaching and the new technology. Large-screen projectors, slide shows and multi-media backdrops have been added to acoustic communication. More than twenty years ago, the Catholic bishops of the United States published *Environment and Art in Catholic Worship* (Washington: United States Catholic Conference, 1978), in which they suggested that audio-visual equipment might have a part to play in public worship (104–106) without, however, reducing the congregation to a passive audience of spectators. Other voices have also called for seeing the sermon and preaching the picture (Eldon Weisheit, *A Sermon is More than Words* [St. Louis: Concordia Publishing House, 1977]; Jean Chollet, "Prédication et Narration," *Foi et Vie* 85/ 2–3 [April 1986]: 35–49). Perhaps it is time to reevaluate our Sunday morning means of announcing the Good News. There is ample historical evidence that others before us have thought likewise. As we have seen, in the Hispanic tradition, the witness of the eyes was of particular importance during the centuries of the first evangelization and it lives on today in popular piety and personal religiosity (Segundo Galilea, *Religiosidad Popular y Pastoral Hispano-Americana* [New York: Centro Cátolico de Pastoral para Hispanos, 1981]).

The three great movements of the sixteenth-century—the Reformation, the Counter-Reformation and the evangelization of America—followed close on the heels of the new technology of printing. The revolution of black type on white paper gave the impression that the Word could become text, but I have attempted to show that the more catholic and Catholic tradition is that the Word has become image. At the start of a new millennium, when the church has called for a second evangelization, we have begun to re-value the icons of our faith and open our eyes to the optical impact of the incarnation. The signs of the times call us to move beyond the verbose and the prolix, and to encounter the Divine *Logos* in new ways—he who is the *vera icon* (true image) of the Father.

Juan J. Sosa

Preaching and Popular Religion

Hispanic popular piety, though
historically often separated
from preaching, offers a concrete,
dramatic way to proclaim and
embody the message of the gospel.

On first impression, the two concepts, preaching and popular religion, though dynamic in the pastoral life of the church, appear to be
contradictory or opposite. Some might take them in a literal sense,
namely, preaching as homiletics, and popular religion, best known
as popular religiosity or piety, strictly as devotional.

Indeed, as we look at both concepts from a historical perspective,
a disparity, more than a correlation, seems to surface. Preaching has
always described the very nature of the church. From earliest times,
preaching was the heartbeat of the announcement and transmission
of Christ's Good News or *kerygma* (as seen in, among other places,
the Acts of the Apostles). Later, through the work of religious communities, it became an effective means to eradicate doctrinal errors,
ambiguity in the teachings of the church and even heresy. Finally,
within the ritual structure of each of the church's liturgical celebrations, preaching has always played a special role in the celebration
of the sacraments and, in particular, the Sunday eucharist. Popular
religiosity, on the other hand, seems to have surfaced from the *sensus fidelium* (sense of the faithful), from the spiritual needs of people
who longed to express the mysteries of the Lord in their own

language and with their own cultural symbols. Popular religiosity or religion became more divergent when such mysteries, well preserved in European monasteries and cathedrals, were celebrated in a language foreign to most of the faithful. Popular religious expressions have always been a treasure of prayerful moments and sacred signs that mark the liturgical calendar with joy and exultation, a legacy of devotions handed down from generation to generation as an integral component of the church's tradition.

The aim of this essay is not to provide the reader with a purely historical survey of how these two elements became estranged. Nor is the intent to show how they are being brought together in ritual through the creative endeavors of good pastoral liturgists in response to the Council's call to reform our popular devotions (*Sacrosanctum Concilium*, 13), Pope Paul VI's exhortation to evangelize all people (*Evangelii Nuntiandi*, 48), and the subsequent interest in these religious customs which the Latin American bishops sparked in 1979 in their III Latin American Conference (*Puebla*, 444). My aim is not to relate ongoing pastoral exercises in ritual creativity built on ecclesial tradition, but rather to examine the key elements which both the preaching of the church and the ongoing religious practices of popular devotions share. In this analysis, I believe we will discover the strength of our tradition in offering meaning to a world deprived of purpose; we will also find the ingredients for the new evangelization to which Pope John Paul II calls us in the third millennium.

PROCLAMATION: THE KEY TO PREACHING THE WORD

If we accept language as the key mechanism for the communication of meaning (Aylward Shorter, *Evangelization and Culture* [New York: Geoffrey Chapman, 1994]), we should begin to expand our concept of preaching to other forms of communication beyond the homily or even the sermon. The paschal mystery has been proclaimed through the ongoing catechetical activity of missionaries throughout the world, the printing of the word in books and articles, and even the conversations that Christians share on an informal daily basis. Once we accept preaching first as proclamation, then we are bound to consider non-verbal forms of proclamation as integral to the efforts toward evangelizing others and ourselves.

One of these forms is that of the *image*, the non-verbal proclamation of Jesus' Good News. Widely used for centuries in the East
as a teaching tool that uttered the word in the colorful mosaics of
ancient basilicas, or captured in paintings and statues certain aspects
of the mysteries of Christ in a non-narrative form, images became
translated over time into more poetic and musical forms of expression, such as the Christian theater and even sacred dance. Without
these forms of communication—transformed into images—the
Good News of Jesus Christ could neither find acceptance by nor
become acceptable to many cultural groups throughout the world.
More than images that arise out of the word proclaimed or written,
these other images that appeal to the senses but aim at reaching the
human heart communicate the depth of all meaning, an authentic
encounter with the Risen Lord, who has come "not to condemn the
world, but to save the world" by sharing his peace with all, especially the poorest and weakest among us (John 3:17).

The verbal or non-verbal proclamation of the paschal mystery,
namely, the death and resurrection of the Lord, could fall into a
vacuum unless those who hunger to listen to its message commit
themselves to living it without question or doubt. For the proclamation of the Good News should lead us all to living it uncondi-
tionally, even if all of its demands become arduous and troublesome
at times. More than ever in a world that struggles to maintain international peace without much success, the poor of the gospel,
reflected in the many hungry, homeless and displaced of society,
confront us beyond our expectations and challenge us to bring to
them the same meaning enshrined in the word proclaimed through
words and images. Unfortunately, they do not find in many of the
people who claim to live the word a message of liberation from
their conditions of chaos; those who followed Jesus found in him
just such a message in the first century. Perhaps, as we listen to and
proclaim the word daily, we are not convinced enough that we need
to become the very word that we proclaim in words or images.

Some claim that this proclamation has become merely a comfortable exercise that avoids confronting the misery of humankind with
the healing and compassionate strength of the Christ who dwells
among us as church and who alone can transform it by announcing
liberty to captives and freedom to the oppressed (Luke 4:18). When

we decide to opt entirely for what Jesus opted for and preferred in his ministry, maybe our world will be different and our ongoing proclamation of his word will shed its "light to those who live in darkness and the shadow of death" (Luke 3:79).

POPULAR RELIGION AS A PROCESS
FOR SYMBOLIC COMMUNICATION

Popular religion is often described in anthropological writings as "folk religion." Visually expressed with color and movement, folk religious rituals are a rich source of investigation and analysis, outlining a unique avenue of expression in the rites of passage of tribal societies (Victor W. Turner, *The Ritual Process: Structure and Anti-structure* [New York: Cornell University Press, 1969]). During these rites, candidates who are eligible for new roles within the tribal structure become separated from their ordinary rhythm of existence in order to experience *communitas* (a state of homogeneity or equality with all other candidates) through a liminal phase in which all the secrets about their new role and their self-worth or identity as members of the tribe are affirmed through a continuous transmission of their specific cultural values, transformed and organized as dominant or instrumental symbols; only after this liminal phase of *communitas* can they become incorporated once again into the rhythm of tribal reality, after embracing and assuming a new role assigned to them by societal leaders.

This ritual process of a balanced social order, which has found a special place in the writings of symbolic anthropologists, has likewise been applied—to a certain degree—to contemporary cultural groups in search of cultural adaptation. A new ethnicity seems to arise out of the need of cultural groups to separate themselves from the ordinary rhythm of life to experience the key ingredients of their cultural heritage, so that, reinforced and affirmed by their own traditions, they can return to their everyday activities and contribute to the larger and complex society in which they live.

In our urban centers, this anti-structural process first discovered in tribal experiences is best seen in community celebrations and feasts, which mark the civic calendar with great expectations by all (for example, parades, local celebrations, athletic competitions,

open-air concerts). At these moments, the complexity of urban living
seems to be relaxed for a day, or at least for a few hours, to give way
to a homogeneous experience of joyful festivities as in a liminal or
pseudo-liminal phase of community building. Moreover, outside of
these civic celebrations, some writers have claimed to discover the
same pseudo-liminal phase in the festive celebrations of popular
religion enjoyed for centuries within the tradition of the Catholic
church, such as pilgrimages to such well-known sites as the Holy
Land, Mont-St.-Michel in France, Compostela in Spain, Rome in
Italy, and the processions that capture the spiritual mood of participants during Holy Week and other significant moments of the liturgical calendar (Victor and Edith Turner, *Image and Pilgrimage in
Christian Culture* [New York: Columbia University Press, 1978]).

At these religious festivals, popular religion provides the participants with an anti-structural experience in which they feel as one,
in a homogeneous setting bound by a common goal of worship, far
distant from the socio-economic classifications or distinctions that
separate them and differentiate them in the structural marketplace.
At these moments, faith finds its way from the mind to the heart
and makes itself evident in poetry, music and dancing, for the quality of the sacred no longer belongs to the few, but is rather in pos-
session of the many. These occasions, which celebrate God's power
and strength, gently touch the participant through a variety of signs
and symbols. Indeed, at these festive celebrations, the rich treasure
of Catholic symbols is communicated to the faithful with power and
beauty. The faithful, in turn, seem to experience a definite Catholic
identity that, some claim, has become absent from the lives of many
in the post–Vatican II era. As a point of clarity, my understanding of
popular religiosity is in line with that of Pope Paul VI, who wrote
that it was the "particular expressions of the search for God and for
the faith, both in the region where the church has been established
for centuries and where it is in the course of becoming established."
These expressions of the faith, often considered less pure and even
despised by many, are today being rediscovered (Sosa, "Liturgical
Piety or Popular Piety? An Anglo-Hispanic Dilemma," *Liturgy* 23/6
[November–December 1979]).

Most certainly, the majority of Catholics would not articulate the
process outlined above in such terms, but they certainly live out

how the process functions within the structures of society to such a degree that their closeness to popular religion sometimes surpasses or substitutes for that of the official worship of the church, such as the Sunday eucharist. While this proposition needs further investigation and reflection, we need to remember that the best-attended church liturgies throughout a given year seem to be governed by the most colorful and significantly expressive celebrations that surround the mysteries of the incarnation (Nativity and Epiphany) and redemption (Ash Wednesday, Holy Week, Easter). These celebrations do not limit the cultural or religious expressions of the people, but rather expand them into a tapestry of multiple religious practices that move beyond the constraints of a church building into the people's homes (for example, *posadas*, nine days of representations of Mary and Joseph searching for an inn at which to rest on Christmas Eve; *pastorelas*, dramatic and musical representations of various Nativity scenes; and *aguinaldos*, early morning Masses during the novena prior to Christmas Day, after which Christmas carols accompany a fine breakfast at a neighbor's home) or even the streets (for example, the distribution of ashes outside of the church, the outdoor Way of the Cross, Good Friday processions and even Easter egg hunts).

Closely related to these major seasons of the year, three specific moments seem to capture the imagination and the heart of the faithful in various ways: the blessing of candles at the opening rite of the Feast of the Presentation (February 2), the blessing of throats on the feast of Saint Blase (February 3), and the blessing and distribution of palm branches at the opening rite of Passion Sunday (Ash Wednesday has already been mentioned). Supported by descriptive narratives that vividly describe the reason for the particular blessing, the acts of blessing and distribution seem to prevail over the enunciated texts and, thus, the symbols that stand out as the focus of each blessing become more intimately appreciated by the faithful than the actual meaning that the symbols convey.

A crucial question arises: Can the ensemble of these symbolic and communitarian experiences known as popular religion, religiosity or piety become an avenue of proclamation of God's word? In other words, do the faithful proclaim the mysteries and the joys of the revealed word of God at the popular celebrations of the liturgical calendar? If not, what are they actually proclaiming?

POPULAR RELIGION AS PROCLAMATION OF THE WORD AND FAITH EXPERIENCE

As in Hegelian dialectic, I have first attempted to present the function of preaching as a thesis, which may provide us with many questions. I have introduced the concept of popular religion as its antithesis. It is time now to bring together these concepts into a synthesis that presents the word as proclaimed and as lived out by those who, though living their faith on many occasions at the margin of the official worship of the church, experience the meaning of the same faith both in a domestic environment and in the community experience provided by popular religion.

For the sake of clarity, I will divide these religious practices into three areas that address this synthesis: First, popular religion as actively proclaiming the paschal mystery outside the liturgy and in small communities. Second, popular religion as the embodiment of church through the living out of the gospel by church people. Third, the blessings of the church as the ongoing affirmation of God's continuing assistance and company to God's people.

The passion, death, resurrection and ascension of the Lord—or the paschal mystery—has found visual and verbal expression among the faithful through the Way of the Cross and the recitation of the mysteries of the rosary. Both practices point to the proclamation of a message enshrined in the concepts of journey and repetitive prayer. As in other religious experiences born and sustained at the margin of the official liturgy of the church, these devotional practices contain within their ritual structure the elements of proclamation. No wonder the Constitution of the Sacred Liturgy called for their renovation (13), which has ultimately led these two Catholic rituals to enhance what they already contain in capsule form with sections of the scripture. The restoration of scriptural rosaries and the popular addition of the Resurrection as the fifteenth Station of the Cross are evidence of such efforts. Within the same timeframe as the liturgical reform, the renewal of these devotions has been widely received by the faithful without much question or doubt, perhaps because each of these devotions already contained elements of the word (specifically the New Testament) before well-intentioned catechists or liturgists added more sections of the scriptures to enhance them. In essence, all the stories about Our Lady point directly to the mysteries of the Lord as celebrated by the church. At the popular celebrations of these mysteries, a sense of the sacred in images and relics seems to take a more prominent place than the assent to doctrinal formulae or credal beliefs; the artistic and tangible, then, embody the tradition of the church in ways that can inspire the faithful to believe. As the heart is touched, the mind requires a form of expression that can only come later, with appropriate catechesis.

In the multiple sacred experiences that highlight the celebrations of the Blessed Mother and the patronal feasts of the saints (that is, processions, novenas, *tridua* and *romerías*), the faithful identify with the lived experience of the word (namely the incarnate presence of Jesus' paschal mystery) in those whom they venerate. Mary, then, embodies the trust of the faithful who commit themselves to surrender their will to God's will, as she did, instead of placing their trust in psychics or seers. Old Testament prophecy and New Testament discipleship find an avenue of expression in these experiences that help the faithful remember the selfless love of Jesus, who inspires them to live, die and rise as he did. The saints, more than intercessors, become the men and women of all times and places who dared shape their lives around the living presence of their Savior and who were not afraid to give up those lives for the meaning that the Savior—through the church—brought to them. In popular religion or piety, the stories of the saints embody the living gospel of the Lord in ways that poorly celebrated liturgies, official as they are, do not. The challenge, of course, is for those responsible for maintaining these celebrations to keep them oriented always toward the paschal mystery, and never to allow mediocrity or poor taste to rob the celebrations of their beauty and power. After all, it is this communion of saints that we mention in our Creed and in which we, the church on its way to eternity, rejoice and find meaning and hope for the journey.

Thirdly, the revision of the *Book of Blessings* has provided pastoral agents with two formidable elements: the inclusion of God's word in every blessing, simple and short as it may be, and the recitation of prayers that focus on those who request the blessing—the faithful—more than on the objects to be blessed (that is, houses, cars, medals, statues, scapulars, rosaries, sacred vessels, and so on). Such innovations place the action of God within human reach, the Lord ever present to his people, both assuring them of his company and challenging them to live out their baptismal commitment. In the blessings which many of our faithful request lie a wealth of opportunities to proclaim the message of salvation as proclaimed by God's living word. In the sacramentals that the church celebrates throughout the year, we encounter the ongoing need to express our faith and to strengthen it with the word that brings light to our actions and proclaims the Good News of the Lord Jesus in the midst of the cultural bad news that so often surrounds us. Ordained ministers, in particular, are called upon to incorporate the word into every sign and symbol in the sacred rituals. Blessings, while helping the faithful to come in touch with transcendence in a unique manner, require of the ordained minister the specific task of communicating the divine presence of our God among those who seek him out through images and objects. What a privileged position: to help believers focus on their conversion through the image they venerate and to translate it back into the word it is called to represent!

CONCLUSION

Do many of the religious devotions that characterize our Catholic tradition contain the dynamism of proclaiming God's word? The answer is yes. Popular religion can become a preaching tool to the degree that it proclaims, more than in words, in signs, gestures, movements and attitudes (for example, the sacrifice of moving out of ordinary existence) the saving act of God who sent his only son to redeem the world and not to condemn it (John 3:16–17). Usually nurtured and displayed by the humble of heart—and on many occasions by the poorest and the weakest among us—popular religion is not only a way of proclaiming and preaching the word, but a way of living out the demands to which this very proclamation calls us. In fact, the authenticity of faith expression and faith experience is often best evidenced by the many who live out the gospel at home more frequently than in church. Those who attend church regularly sometimes lose interest in the dynamics of participation, unless they are provided with the power, the strength and the challenges of good preaching.

Such an observation, however, is not aimed at calling our faithful to abandon church attendance and to limit their faith expression to the home or to infrequent moments in the liturgical calendar. On the contrary, it is aimed at challenging us to see beyond the obscurity with which, at times, we envision the popular expressions of our faithful and to consider them as a true challenge to our everyday experience of God in our personal or communal spirituality. We are all called to preach the word, to communicate its saving message, to live out its transforming experience. Let us work together to make this proclamation the source of our true preaching in words, signs and gestures that echo the compassionate presence of God in our lives. Let us dare find it in the poorest and weakest among us. Above all, let us dare discover the power of his word among those who live it out in humble ways, perhaps without theological sophistication, but with much passion and excitement over the Good News that it proclaims.

Raúl Gómez, SDS

Preaching the Ritual Masses among Latinos

*Ritual celebrations and the family
are at the heart of Latino sacramental
relations and events, as illustrated
in a recent movie.*

BACKGROUND

I have developed a practicum course called "Presiding and Preaching in the Hispanic Community," geared toward seminarians at Sacred Heart School of Theology who will be ministering in a Latino setting in the United States. Although the primary focus is simply to learn how to preside at the eucharist in Spanish, throughout the semester I introduce my students to other significant liturgical events that they will encounter as they minister in the various Latino communities. Some of these celebrations, though following the liturgical system of the Catholic church, include important variations of which these seminarians need to be aware. These liturgies are the key rituals of the church amplified by certain characteristic faith expressions of Hispanic cultures. They include baptism, the presentation of a three-year-old, first communion, the *quince años* (a young woman's fifteenth birthday), weddings and funerary practices. I also provide my students with foundational principles for presiding and preaching among Hispanics. In this essay I will discuss three important principles which all need to have in mind when preaching the ritual masses among Latinos. Following this, I will explain three markers or characteristics of the cultural context of Latinos and Latinas.

FIRST PRINCIPLE: RELIGIOUS EXPERIENCE

The first principle is: Connect those who are hearing you with their own religious experience. I use the example of the Inuit, who have about fifteen terms for snow. I ask my students: "Why would the Inuit need to have so many terms to describe a concept for which we use only one word?" Clearly it is because snow is so significant to them. They need to know what is good, safe snow, and what is dangerous, troublesome snow. In this way, these terms become markers for a particular worldview, in this case one in which how to manage and live in snow is paramount. The use of special terms for the specific types of snow connects the Inuit to their world and experience.

This can be applied to any culture, including Latinos. We too have specific markers that reveal a certain worldview. I submit that the Hispanic worldview is centered on our religious experience. Our faith proclaims a gracious God who manifests himself in various ways both in nature and in human beings, in the saints and in the liturgy, in the Virgin and in our mothers, in word and in sacrament, in food and in music. Some of the identifying markers of this worldview are our devotion to the Virgin and the saints; the Day of the Dead and the novena for the dead; the importance of baptisms, first communions, and *quince años*; the use of *altarcitos* (home altars), *novenarios* (novenas), *milagritos* (ex votos), and candles; wedding practices such as the *lazo* (yoke) and *arras* (coins).

SECOND PRINCIPLE: COMMUNICATION

One way to address the presence of these markers is to examine how Hispanics draw conclusions. This is related to the second principle: Know who your audience is and what they expect to hear. This will facilitate communication as well as provide an opportunity to make connections to an audience's religious experience. In order to examine this principle, I engage my students in an exercise that involves

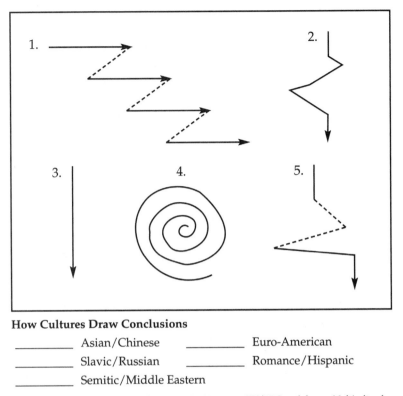

How Cultures Draw Conclusions

_____ Asian/Chinese _____ Euro-American

_____ Slavic/Russian _____ Romance/Hispanic

_____ Semitic/Middle Eastern

Diagrams adapted from presentation by Dr. Marina Herrera at ATS/URC workshop on Multicultural Education, Chicago, December 1, 1989.

a worksheet containing five diagrams. These were developed by Dr. Marina Herrera and presented at an Association of Theological Schools' Under-Represented Constituencies workshop on Multicultural Education held in Chicago in 1989. I have adapted them slightly (see above). Students are asked to match the drawings to the names of five general cultural groups. These are Asian/Chinese, Euro-American, Romance/Hispanic, Semitic/Middle Eastern, and Slavic/Russian.

Very often the students correctly identify the Euro-American diagram (number 3). This style of communication is represented by direct, straightforward speech in which a premise is presented, supported by evidence and affirmed by a conclusion that follows from the premise. The goal of this type of communication is the provision of manageable bits of data that can be digested quickly and can lead to certain action or knowledge. I suggest this style of communication values precision, efficiency and the productive use of time. Communication content is more important than contact, and reflects what Edward Hall calls Low Context communication (Edward Hall, *Beyond Culture* [New York: Anchor Books/Doubleday, 1989]).

The Romance/Hispanic model is more difficult to identify. My students usually associate it with either numbers 5 or 4. They suggest that Hispanics tend to speak in a circuitous manner, which these diagrams appear to illustrate. According to Herrera, the correct answer is 2 because it represents a style of communication in which the interlocutor begins at a certain point and begins to develop it. As he or she continues, another point is brought in, which somehow is related to the primary point. This may then remind the speaker of yet another point, which eventually draws the speaker back to the main idea and leads to the conclusion. One eventually reaches the conclusion, although the route to it is through related detours of thought. I venture to say that this style of communication, in addition to conveying data and knowledge, fosters connection and relationship between the interlocutors. In other words, contact is more important than content and reflects High Context communication (Hall). Perhaps this is one reason why it often takes more words to say things in Spanish than in English. The more time we spend together, the better chance that barriers will come down and a relationship can be established.

As for the other diagrams, number 1 refers to Semitic/Middle Eastern communication in that it captures the use of interconnected stories that illustrate the same point. Much like the serial parables of Jesus, one can come in at any time and get the point, which is then reinforced by another illustration that communicates a worldview. Number 4 is Slavic/Russian and has much in common with the Romance/Hispanic in that one thought leads to another, although each piece has a life of its own. However, when one reaches the conclusion, it is different from where one thought the conversation was going. It is not until one looks back that one can see how the pieces are interrelated, as in a Russian novel. For example, in the novel *Anna Karenina*, the main character has a variety of names to be used depending on the situation, and appears to be respectively different persons, until it is revealed that she has always been the same complex individual. Number 5 is Asian/Chinese and should be seen as if it were a three-dimensional drawing. Asian languages akin to Chinese carry nuances that are layered on top of each other depending on intonation and context. For one not knowledgeable, these languages can seem impenetrable, although they carry a depth of meaning that is uncovered as communication takes place.

Obviously these diagrams and their interpretations can be taken as a form of stereotyping. Nonetheless, they are meant to be points of departure for further reflection and discussion on what values are communicated by the way different cultures reach conclusions. There are also obvious limits in this exercise in that neither the African American nor Amerindian is represented in this worksheet. Therefore, I use other materials in the practicum to address these, since their cultural traits form part of Latino cultures as well.

THIRD PRINCIPLE: HISPANIC SACRAMENTALITY

The ritual masses developed by the Roman Catholic church mark key rites of passage that not only signify the movement of human beings through life, but also provide and celebrate a certain encounter with God's action and grace in life, an encounter that is culturally mediated. Therefore, the third principle is: Name God's action and grace in this particular event for this particular people.

The experience of the supernatural and the numinous in our lives can be called sacramentality. Hispanic sacramentality, while rooted in the celebration of the sacraments, goes beyond them to lift up an experience of God's action and grace that is deeply linked to the Latino world view. This is why the main sacramental events identified by the church are amplified by collateral celebrations developed by Hispanics.

Vatican II's reform of the liturgy has prompted theologians to reexamine the notion of sacramentality. This reexamination, which began already before the Council, has resulted in a questioning of traditional categories and methods of discussing the sacraments. Part of the reason is the introduction of local languages and customs into the liturgy (see Peter E. Fink, SJ, "Sacramental Theology after Vatican II," *The New Dictionary of Sacramental Worship* [College-ville: The Liturgical Press, 1990]). Because of new approaches to sacraments occasioned by the Council, traditional concepts of effi-cacy, causality, matter, form, liceity, validity, symbol, sign and grace no longer capture the whole of what the church is trying to name by sacrament. In addition, extensive development in terms of theolog-ical methods, modes of discourse and paradigms has made it very difficult to synthesize notions of sacramentality into a coherent sacramental theology.

Although this brief piece cannot adequately develop these three principles, I offer three main markers that point to sacramentality in the specific cultural context of the Latino. They include sacramental relationships, sacramental events and characteristics of Hispanic sacramentality. Each of these must be kept in mind when preaching the ritual masses among Latinos.

FIRST MARKER: SACRAMENTAL RELATIONSHIPS

Relationships among Hispanics tend to be hierarchical and very structured. People are addressed with respect and those with authority or advanced age are given honorific titles such as *Don* and *Doña*. These persons are invested with much power and responsi-bility for subordinates. In addition, efforts are made to transform potentially difficult relationships into a network of potentially bene-ficial ones by means of *compadrazgo* (ritual kinship) formalized by such sacramental events as a baptism, a *quince años,* or a wedding. In my judgment, this network of relationships is a crucial factor in discerning a Latino experience of sacramentality.

As a way to illustrate this marker with my students, I make reference to the movie, *The Milagro Beanfield War* (Robert Redford and Esparza Moctesuma, producers; based on the novel by John Nichols; screenplay by David Ward and John Nichols; distributed by MCI Home Video, 1988). There is a scene in which a young soci-ologist, Herbie Platt, encounters old Don Almarante Córdova remonstrating with someone whom the young man cannot see. The audience has known all along that some sort of spirit has been visit-ing the elderly gentleman, preparing him for the coming conflict in the village of Milagro, New Mexico. Although the other villagers take it for granted he talks to a saint or an angel, only Don Almarante sees the gray-bearded man dressed in sombrero, red serape, white shirt, pants and sandals, and who plays a squeeze box. The spirit tends to be mischievous and appears unexpectedly at key moments of the drama. Is he an angel, Saint Jude, God?

Later Herbie asks Don Almarante about the small statue he has noticed. Don Almarante takes down Saint Jude, Patron of Desperate Causes, from his altar and explains that he would have been dead long ago if it was not for the saint's help. Dubious, Herbie questions him how this is possible. Don Almarante proceeds to explain that people have forgotten how to talk to saints . . . or angels: "You have to put up a nice meal, some salsa, tamales, maybe a little beer; then you talk about what you need." In other words, on occasion even the saints and angels need good food and drink, a little conversation and prodding to do what is right. Later, when the venerable don is wounded by a gunshot, the young sociologist turns to Don Almarante's statue, offering food and beer in a humorous but at the same time serious attempt to save his life.

The scenes I have described are an accurate depiction of typical attitudes about the supernatural and the experience of the numinous among some Hispanics. There is a sense that God is immanently accessible, especially to certain people and in particular events. These people include the family, the innocent, the elderly and mothers. Furthermore, God is accessible in the events of home life, suffering, prayer and celebration. In my analysis, these categories are part of the key to ascertaining what sacramentality might be and how it may function in a Latino context. Since family, innocents and motherhood make up key aspects of this first marker, I will say a few words about each.

Family   Latinos tend to work toward creating *familia*. This does not refer to nuclear relationships alone, nor even just to immediate relatives, but it can include friendships and even the *barrio* or neighborhood. Often there is a preference for establishing the closest friendships within the family structure: best friends are commonly siblings or cousins. The links established among relatives are expressed in unique kinship terms: First cousins, for example, are *primo hermano/a* (cousin-brother/sister). The spouses of sisters-in-law or brothers-in-law are *concuños*.

Supposedly from our Amerindian heritage comes the concept that people are born "faceless"; through incorporation into the group they receive a face or personhood. As a consequence, at times Hispanics have trouble relating well to others who are not of "our" group. As mentioned earlier, this is often overcome through *compadrazgo*. Furthermore, there is a perception that if one is alienated from one's own group, there is a loss of personhood.

The Innocent   There are certain people who are perceived to be especially close to God. These include *los inocentes* (the innocent). For instance, in *The Milagro Beanfield War,* there is a woman who is evidently mentally retarded. She has a nasty habit of tossing pebbles at people from behind a wall. Although at times the villagers tell her to stop, they tolerate her, presumably because she is not responsible for her actions. She is "innocent," that is, harmless, and thus under God's special care. As a consequence, she is to be accepted as she is, however bothersome.

Those perceived to be closer to God because of their innocence are sometimes small children. Parents tend to exhibit much tolerance as their children explore or make noise, even at worship. Because of their innocence, it is said they are close to God: They have not yet experienced sin. With time, discipline will come from life experience. Thus children are often doted upon and admired as seeds of promise, of betterment, of a glorious future. For example, parents often call their children *mi rey/reina, mami/papi, mi amor* (my king/queen, mommy/poppy, my love), and so on. Perhaps due to the importance of the group, either as a family or a community, it is regularly thought that when children are successful, their parents are successful; when children fail, parents fail. This obviously places much stress, in all senses of that word, on relationships.

The Elderly   There are still others perceived to be closer to God. These are old people, especially our *abuelitos/as* (grandparents). This is based on the logic that through the normal course of their lives they have had much suffering and hardship, and many experiences that have given them wisdom. This gives them a special place in the *familia* by which they are able to guide and help understand the meaning of life. Also, because they are at the end of their life, there is a sense that they are closer to God and therefore, to eternal life. As a result, they are thought to have a deeper spirituality that can help one see God's action in the midst of life's struggles. This is a scene in the film when Herbie Platt asks Joe Mondragón about Don Alma-rante. Having overheard the elderly gentleman, the oldest man in Milagro, remonstrating with someone who "obviously was not there," Herbie asks Joe if Don Almarante is mentally sound. Joe responds nonchalantly, "He was probably talking to a saint . . . or an angel."

Mothers   A primary person who may help identify a Hispanic sense of sacramentality is the mother. She is at the center of most Latino families. As the fount of physical life she has propagated the family, carrying, nurturing and protecting the offspring inside herself. She is the symbol par excellence of the family. It is the mother who makes one a person. She teaches civility and she hands on the faith, values and attitudes that remain with one throughout all of life. In other words, she is the primary transmitter of Hispanic culture. The worst insult that can be made to Hispanics is to insult or curse their mother. A sign of her status is that the Latina never loses her surname. She will always retain it and hand it on to her children along with that of her husband. Also, when a woman marries, she becomes the owner of the house and receives the title of *ama de casa* ("master" of the house). Although she may put her children first, she is the center of the family. I attribute this to what Ana María Díaz-Stevens calls the "matriarchal core" of Hispanic culture ("Latinas and the Church," *Hispanic Catholic Culture in the U.S.: Issues and Concerns,* ed. Jay P. Dolan and Allan Figueroa Deck, sj [Notre Dame: University of Notre Dame Press, 1994]).

Nonetheless, it is not necessary for a woman to have had chil-dren in order to be a mother. Certain other women can fulfill this role. For instance, in the film, Ruby Archuleta, a single woman, is the energetic owner of a garage who organizes her village into a force with which to be reckoned and represents well Hispanic motherhood: sure, motivating, forceful, insistent and life-giving. Another example of this is that among Latinos women religious are given the title of *Madre* (Mother).

THE SECOND MARKER: SACRAMENTAL EVENTS

The second of the three main markers for identifying Hispanic sac-ramentality and which must be kept in mind when preaching the ritual masses has to do with sacramental events. These events are home life, suffering, prayer and celebration. *The Milagro Beanfield War* illustrates well these points.

Home Life   I detect four spheres of influence that play a decisive role in Hispanic culture. They are the spiritual, material, social and domestic spheres. It seems that the heart of Hispanic culture is where all four spheres intersect. For this reason, permeating much of what Hispanics value is home. Home is at the center of the Hispanic universe. Society is secondary in that its purpose is to support home life. Into the social and domestic spheres Hispanics tend to integrate life and death, that is to say, the material and spiritual worlds. They are not separated out—they are a totality. Thus, Hispanics seem to sense they can and do communicate with God, with saints, with the dead and vice versa. This notion is further reinforced by the use of *altarcitos* and domestic practices centered on popular piety that take place at important intervals throughout the year or even the day.

A possible emblem of this reality is the *ojo de dios* (eye of God) (see *Ojo de Dios* [pamphlet, San Antonio: Mexican American Cultural Center]), a Huichol prayer altar comprising two poles in the shape of a cross and bound together by the weaving of thread. The center, where the two poles intersect, is said to be God's eye. This is where one has access to the sacred realm. As a result, I suggest that at the center of Latino reality is the sacred, encountered at the intersection of the four spheres. It is here where the mother reigns.

Suffering   Suffering is another aspect that is accepted as part of normal life. For instance, Hispanics appear to relate especially well to the incarnated God, Jesus who has suffered as we do, *el nazareno* (the Nazarene), the one condemned to death. For many, the moment of death is holy, a moment of blessing. As a result, there is an attempt to be present at the dying of loved ones. Perhaps a reason for this is a highly developed sense of the sacred, a sense of an intermingling of the spiritual and the material worlds. Maybe this is due to belief in the resurrection of Jesus Christ and the believer's share in it that seems to be deep-seated. Consequently, there is a desire to be present when loved ones go through the door to the fullness of life. There is a saying that this life is but a dream; our dying is waking from the dream. Thus, if at all possible there is an attempt to ask for the loved one's blessing before he or she dies so that those present can also have a share in the grace the dying person is believed to be receiving.

Furthermore, for Hispanics it seems very important not to be alone, especially at significant times of life, including death. We are to accompany our loved ones so that they will have courage and serenity. This "accompanying" continues after death with the "novena for the dead," a nine-day gathering of family and friends in the deceased's home, when praying the rosary and sharing symbolic food such as *pan dulce* (sweet rolls) is important. In this way the memory of the deceased is kept alive. It also serves to help family members feel that they are part of a community that accompanies them in their sorrow.

It has been said that there are three moments of death: the physical, corporal death, the burial, and, finally, when there is no longer anyone to remember you. To keep the memory alive, an altar is kept in the home with the family saints on it and photographs of the family's deceased loved ones. Also on home altars are pictures of loved ones in need, perhaps in an attempt to keep them always before God's eyes. And on the Day of the Dead, gravesites are visited as a way to deepen the spiritual connection.

Prayer If these practices are as widespread as they appear to be, they say much about Latino spirituality. And prayer, the third of the sacramental events I am considering, is often expressed in a great variety of practices called "popular religion." There is a sense that for Hispanics, God is a member of the family. God is called *tata Dios* (grandfather God). Furthermore, Jesus is called *Nuestro Padre Jesús* (our father Jesus). The saints are taken as spiritual *compadres* (co-parents or spiritual kin) and individuals are faithfully devoted to one saint over another. As an example of this, Don Almarante expresses his great devotion to Saint Jude, claiming that without his help he would not be alive. Herbie asks him how this is possible and Don Almarante answers simply, "He's a saint!" Devotees rely on the saints' help in hard times and pay them back in gratitude with *mandas* or *promesas* (symbolic sacrificial or penitential acts). Some also make *juramentos* (oaths or agreements) in the presence of a priest or a sacred image, vowing to refrain from some activity or vice for a set period of time. These are taken very seriously and tend to be fulfilled.

The *santos* (saints) are seen as special friends who can help in daily living. It is for this reason, for example, that Don Almarante brings Herbie a statue of Saint Ignatius, whom he claims to be the Patron of Smart People. The *altarcito* is where saints are met. It is where the transcendent God comes to reside with the family, and its members can engage in intimate communication with God.

This deep abiding faith is also well expressed in the Spanish language: It is replete with "God-talk." It contains many expressions that reflect faith, such as *Si Dios quiere* (If God wants), *Jesús!* (bless you), *Ave María!* (goodness!). Even the words for goodbye, *adiós* (God be with you), and thank you, *gracias* (asking that you receive grace/blessings for your kindness), were originally religious expressions. In my opinion, this is one of the reasons why many Latinos wish to maintain the Spanish language.

Celebration   All these notions are brought together in the final sacramental event I consider, the Hispanic celebration. Latinos tend to glory in life and find many occasions to celebrate it. Justo González names *fiesta* (celebration) as a chief element of Hispanic worship (Justo L. González, "Hispanic Worship: An Introduction," in *Alabadle!: Hispanic Christian Worship*, ed. Justo L. González [Nashville: Abingdon Press, 1996]). In particular, fiesta is when the totality of life is brought together. It expresses hope despite suffering. It also expresses some of Latinos' deepest values: family, blessing, good personal relationships, thanksgiving, well-being, community and spirituality.

For fiesta is not fiesta if God has not been invoked or has not convoked it (for example, at baptism, first communion, *quince años*, funerals, and so on). Fiesta is not fiesta if there is no food, an indication that life is worthwhile and we value the others' life by feeding them. Fiesta is not fiesta if there is no music, the sign that problems can be overcome and people can celebrate God's great gift: life. This is the *Misa, Mesa,* and *Musa* quality of Hispanic celebration: A religious event (*misa* or mass) usually gathers Hispanics. There must be food (*mesa* or table), and singing, dancing and declamation (*musa*—the muse) must enliven the gathering. In my assessment, *Misa, Mesa, Musa* (Ovídeo Pecharromán coined this mnemonic device) *qua* fiesta is a principal key to finding the essence of sacramentality in the Hispanic universe.

In sum, in a preconscious way, Hispanics appear to carry this sense, this intuition, that the spiritual world is very available, and as accessible as the material world. I have presented anecdotal evidence for some of what appears obvious to me, although the roles of healers, land, work, ritual and "being" also come to mind. To the extent that this is true, it forms the basis of Hispanic religious experience. It also points to the characteristics of sacramentality operative among many Hispanics. This forms the third marker that needs to be taken into account when preaching the ritual masses among Latinos.

THIRD MARKER: CHARACTERISTICS OF
HISPANIC SACRAMENTALITY

I began with three principles. I have elucidated two markers. These reflect much of what certain theologians have indicated to be characteristics of sacramentality in general. They include the centrality of Christ, the importance of the incarnation, insertion into the life of the Trinity, the creation of meaning and identity, and the encounter with God in the ordinary leading to ethical action. I now present eight examples of this third marker as they appear among Latinos.

Centrality of Christ   Edward Schillebeeckx notes that God is calling a faithful people to life (*Christ the Sacrament of the Encounter with God* [Kansas City, MO: Sheed & Ward, 1963]). He stresses the centrality of Christ in this action and the church's role in continuing Christ's work of salvation. In my judgment, the Hispanic practices here described reflect this. Focus is placed on the Christ of tenderness, weakness, smallness, dependence on others, and suffering that are encountered at the beginning of his life and at the end of his life (Jaime Lara, "Las Imágenes de Jesucristo Populares en Latinoamérica," in *Religiosidad Popular: Las Imágenes de Jesucristo y La Virgen María en América Latina* [San Antonio: Instituto de Liturgia Hispana, 1990]). Thus there is much devotion to the Child Jesus and

to the *nazareno*. This is then echoed in the attitudes toward the innocent and the elderly.

At the same time, many of the themes and motivations of Latino
devotion are intimately linked to the liturgy and the celebration of
the sacraments, such as at baptism, first communion, and funerals.
The use of home altars for prayer is clearly an example of taking
what occurs in church and applying it to a domestic setting. Also,
many Latino devotions cannot be performed alone; they require others, and so in a sense they foster a community that is God's people.

Importance of Incarnation   Karl Rahner indicates the importance
of finding God and human beings together in order to identify the
sacramental (see Geoffrey B. Kelly, ed., *Karl Rahner: Theologian of the
Graced Search for Meaning* [Minneapolis: Fortress Press, 1992]). The
phenomena I have described emanate from an integration of the four
spheres of influence I have delineated earlier, that is, the material/
spiritual and the social/domestic. In this integration, there is a sense
that God and human beings dwell together. For example, Hispanics
seem to value highly religious customs and the Spanish language
because they convey a sense of God's loving accompaniment, a sense
that God is truly God-among-us: Emmanuel. This also promotes a
sense that God is found in everyday affairs.

The Life of the Trinity   Edward Kilmartin shows that sacramentality participates in the life of the Trinity as an expression of the work
of the Spirit who continues Christ's work (Edward Kilmartin, SJ, "A
Modern Approach to the Word of God," *The Sacraments: God's Love
and Mercy Actualized*, ed. Francis A. Eigo, OSA, and Silvio E. Fitti-
paldi, OSA [Villanova, PA: Villanova University Press, 1979]). Furthermore, the sacraments support Christians as they move toward
the Kingdom, that is, the life of the Trinity. This being drawn into
the life of the Trinity is evidenced by means of the relationships that
are fostered and stressed by Latinos. The emphasis on family (as a
larger reality), the activity of accompanying (especially those suffering), and fiesta that brings all of life together, both human and
divine, appear to be manifestations of what Kilmartin describes.

Meaning and Identity   Louis-Marie Chauvet uses linguistic theory
to show how sacraments are symbols that mediate meaning and

identity (Louis-Marie Chauvet, *Symbol and Sacrament: A Sacramental Reinterpretation of Christian Existence*, trans. Patrick Madigan, sj, and Madeleine Beaumont [Collegeville: The Liturgical Press, 1995]). From this perspective, it is evident that the phenomena described also are symbolic. However, in my assessment they not only mediate what is meaningful for Hispanics, that is, family, faith, life, but they also mediate a sense of being God's people which is integral to their identity. One way this is done is by means of the integration of the paschal mystery into every aspect of life including sayings, language, altars, devotions and so forth. Though these may appear sentimental or even superstitious practices at times, they serve to reinforce who Hispanics are in relation to the spiritual world as mediated by the material.

The Ordinary and Ethical Action   Leonardo Boff's emphasis on the ordinary and material as mediators of sacramentality is very evident in the phenomena I have presented (Leonardo Boff, *Sacraments of Life, Life of the Sacraments*, trans. John Drury [Beltsville, MD: The Pastoral Press, 1987]). Boff shows how ordinary objects and events mediate an encounter with God that leads one to ethical action. In Latino experience, one vows by means of *mandas* and *promesas* to do some action that will help the individual grow in Christian commitment and ethical behavior, even if this is framed in terms of personal gain. The use of *alacitas* ("little wings" — tokens of what is being requested) and *milagritos* (ex-votos, charms representing body parts needing healing) point to the ordinary as mediators of sacramentality, a sacramentality that indicates that God is for us and with us, even in our efforts toward personal improvement.

While the five aspects above apply to sacramentality in general and appear in Hispanic cultural phenomena in particular, there are additional elements that emerge in Hispanic culture as well that require elucidation for more effective preaching among Latinos. Among these are the Latino traits of performing actions as meaningful in themselves, the role of suffering, and the centrality of the feminine. These point to a broader sense of sacramentality.

Meaningful Actions   Much of Latino spirituality is marked by ritualization by means of gestures and repetitive acts. For instance, there is a unique way of making the sign of the cross in which a small cross is first traced on the forehead, then over the lips, followed by the breast, and finally a "regular" sign of the cross to complete it. This is called *persignación* and involves *persinarse* (to make the sign of the cross) and *signarse* (to sign oneself with small crosses). At the same time each action is accompanied by a "blessing": *Por la señal de la Santa Cruz, de nuestros enemigos, líbranos Dios nuestro, en el nombre del Padre, y del Hijo, y del Espíritu Santo. Amén* (By the sign of the Holy Cross, from our enemies free us, our God, in the name of the Father, and of the Son, and of the Holy Spirit. Amen). Another aspect of such cultural rituals is the reciting of prayers such as the Our Father, the Hail Mary, and the Glory Be in multiples of three and the repetition of the same action, such as rubbing, shaking or brushing over the same place the equivalent number of times.

The Role of Suffering   There is a saying among Latinos, *no hay mal que por bien no venga* (there is no evil that does not come for some good). It seems to me that this expresses and fosters a great capacity to endure suffering of any type. Furthermore, it places suffering within the realm of good. As the conflict between the villagers of Milagro and the land developers intensifies, for example, the spirit says to Don Almarante that Joe Mondragón is in over his head in terms of what he has begun. Exasperated, Don Almarante says to the spirit, "I thought you were supposed to help." The spirit responds, "I don't help, I give advice. A great sacrifice is required in this situation." It is shortly after this that Don Almarante's pet hog, Lupita, is found rummaging through the beanfield. This enrages Joe, who shoots at her in order to scare her off. Lupita attacks Joe and as he slips, he wounds her. Don Almarante starts shooting at Joe and Joe ends up wounding the elderly gentleman.

At the end of the film, after the villagers have been victorious over the land developers, there is great rejoicing in the field with the priest blessing the harvest, accompanied by eating, singing and dancing to *De Colores*. The final scene has Don Almarante rushing to the fiesta from the hospital, only to meet the spirit, who shows him a shortcut where he will sooner hear more beautiful music. It is a sign that he is dying and an obvious indication that Don Almarante's suffering or life-giving sacrifice was related to the villagers' success.

This sense that suffering leads to good may have a sacramental function among Latinos.

The Feminine   Traditionally, it has been the Latinas who have handed on religious customs. They have known the "right ways" of offering prayers, of organizing feast days and of celebrating rituals. Because of this Arturo Pérez concludes that women have a central role in Hispanic worship (*Popular Catholicism: A Hispanic Perspective* [Washington: The Pastoral Press, 1988]). This is further demonstrated by the fact that it is normally the mother who sets up an *altarcito* in the home where she prays for her family, living and dead, where she leads the household in prayer, and where she mediates God's presence. In effect, she makes the home a domestic church and she is its pastor. In other words, the feminine, especially in terms of motherhood, appears to have a sacramental function.

CONCLUSION

In this article I have briefly presented three principles and three markers or characteristics of Hispanic culture and spirituality that must be considered for effective preaching. This is especially true for preaching the ritual masses among Latinos, for those occasions are key events that lift up and celebrate Hispanic culture, identity and sacramentality. For effective preaching, the preacher must connect Latinos to their religious experience, must know who the audience is and what will help the hearers make this connection. The preacher must have a keen understanding of where, how, and when Latinos encounter God in their lives. By meeting Hispanics where they are, the preacher can then take them beyond, to a greater understanding, and inspire them to finer integration of their faith in life and of their life in faith.

Victor Alvarez

Preaching to *Generación* X

*Heirs of an ancient and complex
culture, young Hispanics have
a distinctive experience of Catholic
faith and great hopes for the future.*

Our first task in approaching another people, another
culture, another religion is to take off our shoes, for the
place we are approaching is holy. Else we may find ourselves treading on another's dream. More serious still,
we may forget that God was there before our arrival.
(Unknown)

INTRODUCTION

Once, in a tiny village of southern Mexico, a new priest arrived to
serve a parish that had an old statue of Saint James astride a horse
slaying Moors. According to legend, during the Spaniards' last bat-
tle against the Moors in Granada, a mounted Saint James appeared
in the sky to help the Spaniards expel the invaders. The Spaniards
later brought this tradition to Mexico. The young priest decided to
change the statue of the parish's patron, and brought in a statue of
the apostle without the horse, without consulting the parishioners.
He wanted to surprise them. When the people arrived for Mass the
next morning, they were indeed surprised, and filled with anger
because the *padrecito* (priest) had changed the most important saint
of all—the horse!

This story is true. The people of that small village used to rub and pray to the genitalia of Saint James' horse, as a rite of fertility. The indigenous people called it the "Holy Force."

This story teaches us about how difficult it is to understand other cultures, especially when we talk about the incarnation of the gospel into a culture. How can we preach to a group as distinct from ourselves as *Generación X?*

GETTING TO KNOW YOU

There is a saying, "If you want to know your country, get out of it." As a Mexican living in the United States, I can say that I have learned more about Mexico since I have lived here than when I was living there. From an objective perspective, I can admire the deep spirituality of the Hispanics living in the United States. "They see God all over the place," a young seminarian once told me, talking about his new experience in Mexico. Hispanics like to invoke the name of God, as well as those of the saints, as protectors in danger-ous situations. "He is a personal God, someone who relates person-ally and directly with His children. Among the attributes and images of God that most often appear is that of a *Father,* the Creator who is a compassionate forgiver, who is providential, who cares—when no one else may seem to. Above all, He is the one who understands. A popular notion among Hispanics is that God even understands sin. On the other hand, God is the supreme lawmaker and judge. In this regard, God is all-knowing, and will punish when we offend Him or our neighbor" (Bishop Ricardo Ramirez, "Hispanic Spiritu-ality," *Social Thought* 9:3 [Summer 1985]).

This does not mean that Hispanics are saints or that their reli-gion is better than anyone else's. What I want to say is that their life is a symbiosis of the pre-Hispanic indigenous cultures and myths, along with the Catholicism brought by the conquistadores. This is a reality for many countries in Latin America. This mixture has cre-ated a new and fascinating Hispanic religious lifestyle in the United States full of ambiguities and paradoxes. As Steve Giorno has said: "Hispanic culture is where faith and 'sound theology' are some-times intertwined with tradition, legend, superstition and popular folklore. This is lived by the Latinos without being perceived as conflictive or contradictory." (University of St. Mary of the Lake, Mundelein Seminary, 1999)

A young Jehovah's Witness once asked me about eschatology. After I finished my comments, thoughts, opinions and dogmas, she said: "Wow! This is beautiful. But it is not what your people really believe. That makes me think that you do not know your parishioners who I visit day by day. Even though some of them reject me, I know their faith." This impressed me so much that every time I have the opportunity to bless a house or to eat with a family or just to visit, I do it with the desire to learn more about them. In preaching, therefore, I can voice their struggles, pains and anxieties as well as their happiness and hopes. I can then offer all of these to our God every Sunday at our communal Mass.

In this essay, I am going to talk about preaching to the new *mestizaje* (mixture) of Latinos in the United States called *Generación X* (Generation X). I will discuss their religious ideas, drawing upon what Rosa María Sánchez and I learned from the "Survey of Young Hispanic Professionals" we conducted in different areas of the United States. We completed this survey under the direction of the National Catholic Council for Hispanic Ministry (NCCHM) with funding from the Koch Foundation.

It is impossible in so brief a presentation to integrate all the Latin American roots and distinct realities, such as those of Cubans, Puerto Ricans, Colombians and Central Americans. Therefore, I will address only the roots of the Mexicans and Mexican Americans, hoping that I can find common threads that may also prove helpful to other Latin American communities.

I will begin by addressing the pre-Hispanic Aztec culture. Then I will examine the roots of the Mexican contributions. This logically leads to a treatment of the Guadalupe phenomenon as a perfect model of *mestizaje*, or the integration of those two different religions and cultures. This necessitates a look at the related phenomena of feminism and machismo. Finally, I will broach the subject of *Generación X* as heirs of this long and complex tradition.

Of course, any of these topics could take an entire book for each. It is my intention to give a general overview of different ways of approaching the confluence of religion, generations and culture in this population. Hispanic reality is complex, including urbanization, education, "North American" influences, media, ethnic diversity and many other elements. I hope that this investigation will help preachers better understand this rich culture as they attempt to preach to young adult Hispanics.

AZTEC CULTURE

Only yellow corn
and white corn were their bodies. . . .
Those who were our fathers
Were the four Original humans.
> (Miguel Leon-Portilla et al., *Native Mesoamerican Spirituality* [New York: Paulist Press, 1980], 123)

Angel Garibay writes about Aztec culture:

Then *Quetzalcoatl* took them [human bones] to *Tamoan-chan*, the land where life is born. Once he arrived, the one who makes the plants grow, *Quilaztli* or *Cihuacoatl*, she ground them on a *metate*. Over them *Quetzalcoatl* poured blood from his loins, after the bath of purification. The rest of the gods did the same. . . . Then they said: 'Gods were born: those are the humans.' The ones who deserved because of the sacrifice. (*Literatura de los Aztecas*, ed. Joaquin Mortiz [Mexico: 1982], 19; my translation.)

That is the legend of how a new race began, the people of the corn, the indigenous of Central Mexico known as Aztecs. Men and women were born from Mother Earth and mixed with god's blood, *chalchichualt* (liquid jewel). These two concepts, the reality of our vulnerability and the awareness of our superiority over creation, were the basis of the Aztec myth of the feathered serpent. *Quetzalcoatl*, besides being a god and a mythological figure, is the image of every human being because his body is anchored to the earth. His feathers represent dreams, illusions, art and spirituality.

MEXICAN CULTURE

When we speak about Mexico or Mexicans, we need to be very specific. Mexico is composed of an incredible diversity of ideas, beliefs, values, practices and wisdom. Even though Mexicans share historic, geographic, religious, racial, linguistic, ethnic and social traditions, they are quite diverse in their cultural expressions. Almost every state or region has its own customs, food, traditions and dances. With this in mind, my intention is not to focus on a certain type of Mexican, but to make reference to the common characteristics that we call Mexican culture.

In 1521, a couple of hundred Spanish soldiers with a few missionaries arrived in a land inhabited by eight million indigenous persons. For Spaniards, "cross and sword" was not a divided concept. Power and religion were very much interconnected, especially after their experience of expelling the Moors, whom they saw as infidels, from Spain.

Cortes and the other Spaniards discovered an impressive culture with highly structured religious practices that were difficult to challenge. The cosmic vision of the Mayas, Toltecs and Aztecs was full of myths and meaning. Cortes, in one of the *Cartas de Relación* (Relating Letters), wrote to the King of Spain that His Majesty needed to send priests who were "saints" because it was impressive how these "Indians" were very religious. The twelve Franciscans who arrived in this new land really were "saints." In only a few years, they "evangelized" the incredibly vast territory from Guatemala to northern California. The way they evangelized was not simple: They learned the different languages of each culture and used the language to teach the basics of the Catholic faith. Charging some people in the community with the care of this faith, the Franciscans proceeded to the next community. Even now in the state of Tlaxcala, one can find lay *mayordomos* (majordomos) in charge of the local church. If they do not fulfill their duties, they have to pay a fine and may even be incarcerated. In this way, the Franciscans made sure that the rules of the Catholic church were present, even though those who made them were not. But rules are made for people, not people for rules. Mexicans tend not to be so tied to the law. European religious practices mixed easily with the indigenous traditions, myths and costumes, creating what we call a Popular Religiosity. A quite different reality emerged in the United States. R. Diaz-Guerrero writes:

> A very different experience occurred here in the United States almost four centuries latter when Puritanism and rigid moral values created the Law as an ultimate symbol of justice and values. . . . At no time did they speak of *fraternity*, as in the slogan of the French revolution. . . . Americans were to be individualistic, independent, competitive, self-initiated and self-reinforced, oriented toward achievement, efficient, and successful, aided by socioeconomic events. This type of thinking flourished and produced a thriving economy. . . . The socioculture rationalized that those who did not take advantage of their equality were inferior, incapable or lazy. . . . The United States of Meso-northamerica is a 'power-equality' socioculture in which affiliation, fraternity, and love, while not completely lacking, are not primary goals. It is this evident lack of fraternity . . . that has caused angry minorities to revolt and seek power. . . . In this socioculture power lies within the individual, while in the socialist sociocultures power lies primarily within the state and secondarily within the people as a whole. (*Psychology of the Mexican, Culture and Personality* [Austin, TX: University of Texas Press, 1976], xiv–xv)

Ignoring the differences between these two cultures has produced misunderstandings and serious conflicts.

In Mexican socioculture, power and love were mixed. The conqueror (the powerful, the male, the Spaniard) mixed with the conquered (the female, the subjugated, the "Indian"). Later, in order to justify enslaving them, some Spaniards concluded that the "Indians" did not have souls. Other Spaniards believed that they could give this soul to the "Indians" by having sexual relations with the indigenous women. This is one of the most powerful and shameful traumas that Mexicans carry with them even to this day. The worst insult to a Mexican is to say that his mother was raped.

Although all power was to be in the hands of the male, all love was to be in the hearts of the female. This is key to understanding

the Mexican family and Mexican socioculture. In Mexico, where in
theory all are equal as far as affection, power is traditionally
bestowed upon those one loves. "This has produced individuals
who are obedient, affiliate, interdependent, orderly, cooperative . . ."
Diaz-Guerrero continues:

> [T]he socioculture of the United States has fostered an
> active way of facing the stress of life . . . to modify the
> environment, whether physical, interpersonal or social. . . .
> The Mexican socioculture . . . seems to feel that the best
> way to resolve problems is to modify oneself . . . rather
> than the environment; he knows many subtle ways of
> dealing with himself. He knows how to modify his
> emotions and his moods. On the other hand, he is quite
> incapable of anticipating the very many details that may
> go wrong when he acts in the physical and economic
> environment. (xviii)

It is important for the preacher to know that in order to engrave
a message in a Hispanic audience, he or she needs to appeal the
heart as well as the brain. The gospel has to be felt through compassion, understanding, care and spontaneous signs of affection before
any series of rules and theologies.

I offer one final comment on Mexican socioculture. Life is not to
be enjoyed, but to be endured. This vision of life has its roots in
early indigenous ways of understanding existence. They believed
that nothing we see would last forever, but that each life had its
destiny already shaped by God and fates. An old man from Vera-
cruz, Mexico, once explained to me: "Since we come to this world to
suffer, we need to really enjoy the few opportunities to be happy."
The joy the Hispanics have has to be shared. It is not individualistic,
but celebrated in community. In that way it becomes more intense.

THE GUADALUPE EVENT AND THE FAMILY

The trauma of the conquest was not only physical or emotional, but
also theological: "Our gods have abandoned us, there is no reason
to live." Although the Aztecs knew almost every medicine to cure
the physical illnesses they had, they were not prepared to face the

spiritual and physical diseases brought by the Europeans. As a result, thousands of indigenous lost their lives to epidemics, slavery and despair.

Catholic evangelization was very difficult. The Aztecs conceded to the new victorious God, but under the Christian crosses they often hid their own gods. They learned to deal with this theological problem by simply saying "yes" to the law and to the priest and then doing their own thing.

Ten years after the conquest, there appeared an image that would join these two religions: To the Spaniards she was the apocalyptic Catholic image of the Virgin, and to the Aztecs she was *Tonanzin* (Our Little Mother). The message from Our Lady of Guadalupe was one of love, dignity, respect and hope, especially for the *mestizos* (the children of the Spaniards and Mexican indigenous) who were caught between these two conflicting religions and therefore lacked any identity of their own. Our Lady's skin color was that of a *mestizo*, and the symbols that surrounded her were in harmony with the most profound theology of the Aztec religion. At the same time, she overshadowed the sun (which the Aztecs worshiped) and called herself the mother of the True God. In her, the opposites were integrated: Mother-virgin, woman-man, conqueror-conquered, good-bad, secular-sacred, native-stranger. She had an important message that transcended language, culture, class, gender, race, theology, logic and reason. Her message was of love and hope beyond all hatred and despair.

Guadalupe was the good news to the poor who had suffered a tremendous humiliation: Their gods were destroyed, their women raped, their truth ignored and their freedom taken away. We can only imagine the confusion of the indigenous people who felt abandoned by their gods. This led to a destruction of their self-esteem, reflected in the dialogue between Juan Diego and the Virgin Mary of Guadalupe. She asked him to be her messenger to the supreme authority, Bishop Fray Juan de Zumarraga. She wanted a "Sacred Little House on which I will show [Jesus], I will exalt him, in making him manifest" (José Luis Guerrero, *El Nican Mopohua, Un Intento de Exégesis* [Universidad Pontificia de México, 1996], 169). The bishop doubted Juan Diego, the native who thought of himself as "[just] a man from the country, I am a [porter's] rope, I am a backframe, a tail, a wing, a man of no importance. . . ." She responded: "Listen, my youngest and dearest son, know for sure that I have no lack of servants, of messengers, to whom I can give the task of carrying my breath . . . but it is very necessary that you, personally, go and plead, that my will become reality." Through this commission, the Virgin gave to Juan Diego the dignity and credibility that no indigenous had had before.

The Virgin wanted the indigenous, who were without hope, to build their own church where she would listen to the lamentations of anyone who wished to come. This is crucial because, although the Aztecs conquered other tribes and sacrificed prisoners of war to the Sun God, they never destroyed other temples. They simply added their own gods. However, the Spaniards destroyed the Aztec temples and built Catholic churches on their ruins. This was the real defeat of the Aztecs, because burning a temple meant the destruction of the state. Therefore, when the Virgin said that she wanted a "Little House," this was the proof of the resurrection of a new race, the continuation of their society in a new era because that was the way they had begun Old Mexico: with a "Little House" for God (Guerrero).

The best representative of a compassionate God was the figure of motherhood. "Am I not here, who is your mother? Are you not under my shadow and protection? Am I not the source of your joy? Are you not in the hollow of my mantle, in the crossing of my arms?"

The image of Guadalupe is so important that it has become the symbol of unity for all Mexicans. It is quite difficult to explain to a Mexican why Catholics do not adore the Virgin, but venerate her. For them, she is the Mother of God who plays a vital role in their lives and history. The image has been present in the most important historical, political and, of course, religious events of the country. The Guadalupe event has influenced the structure of the Mexican family, its spirituality and the way life is perceived.

Most Mexican families are founded upon two fundamental premises: the unquestioned and absolute supremacy of the father and the necessary and absolute self-sacrifice of the mother. Even though this is changing in modern Mexican societies, in terms of sharing more responsibilities in parenthood, the truth is that Mexican families still sense the tremendous influence of these traditions.

The Female Figure   In farming communities, where the land is a symbol of the cycle of life, that which sustains life and to which all will one day return, "mother earth" is sown after prayer. A Mexican man is expected to marry a woman who is a virgin, ideally a "saint," the pure mother of his children. And before consummating the marriage, a prayer may be recited.

In general, women carry the honor of the family. That is why male family members become overprotective of their *mujeres* (women). The family and society allow young women to start dating after their fifteenth birthday, often celebrated with a big fiesta called *Los Quince Años.* In this rite of passage, the girl becoming a woman is the center of attention, and from then until marriage she should be treated like a "goddess" by her suitors. A woman is not usually allowed to move out of the house until she is married. Some families can be very strict in dating matters. They do not give permission to go far from the house, and if her boyfriend enters the house, she has to be with a chaperone. Meanwhile, the boyfriend has to display his best romantic manners (serenades, flowers, poems, presents, and so on) toward the woman in order to get her attention. For men it is important not to fail in this attempt because that reflects badly on their masculinity.

Once a woman is married, the man becomes "the master," and her life may become very difficult until she has children on whom she can project all her care and love. Rosendo Urrabazo sheds light on the topic:

> The authority of the mother in the lives of her children seems to be a reality to be contended with; and only thinly veiled in her self-sacrificing behavior. The desire of children to have their father play an intimate role in guiding them may be a more wished-for event than a reflection of reality. (*Machismo: Mexican American Male Self-Concept* [Ann Arbor, MI: University Microfilms International, 1986], 127)

Machismo   Because much manual labor is needed in farming communities, the male children who perform many of these tasks often have special privileges. However, there are also costs. Men are never to show any kind of weakness such as crying or whining or demonstrating tenderness or sentimentality. Men may show affection toward their children, but without compromising their authoritative role of *consejero* (an advisor or counselor). The mother is the one who takes full responsibility for the household and the children. She is deeply affectionate, tender and overprotective toward the children. In this case, over the power of the *macho*, is the power of the mother. The Oedipus complex, a reality for many Mexicans, results in the idolization of the mother. Diaz-Guerrero writes:

> The extreme separation between the "female set" of values and the "male set," plus the fact that it is the female who teaches and develops the personality of the child, often provokes in the male guilt regarding deviations from the female pattern. Actually, in order to be at ease with the male pattern, he must constantly break with the female one. Perhaps it is not an accident that the main religious symbol is a woman: the Virgin of Guadalupe. From their behavior it appears that the males are caught in a compulsive asking for forgiveness from the same symbol they most betray if they are to be masculine. It is only because a good number succeed in keeping each role distinct and separate . . . that no more or no more serious mental disturbance appears. In many, there is . . . a battle of "superego" and "id," the former representing the mother set of values and the latter the father set. This is a Freudian metapsychology *à la mexicaine*. (12)

Perhaps this is why many male Mexicans look for another woman besides their own wives so that they can somehow escape the Oedipal drama in which they are involved.

Diaz-Guerrero has also written that in the male there may be:

> (a) problems of submission, conflict, and rebellion in the area of authority; (b) preoccupation and anxiety regarding sexual potency; (c) conflict and ambivalence regarding his double role: he must at times love and generally act maternally and tenderly, and at other times act sexually and virilely; (d) difficulties in superseding the maternal stage: dependent-feminine individuals; (e) problems

before and during marriage: mother's love interferes
with the love to another woman (here one should expect
an important area of stress where the husband, the wife,
and the husband's mother play the dynamics of jealousy);
(f) the Oedipus complex, as Freud describes it: almost
every aspect of the ideal setting for its development is
provided by the premises of the culture and the role playing. Actually areas b, c, d, and e above may be considered
as partial expressions of the dynamics of the Oedipus
complex. (10–11)

Machismo is a complicated system of values, rights and feelings. It
involves the family, the society and the religion. The preacher, being
aware of this phenomenon, needs to address it with respect, but
also confront it with gospel values.

An important symbol of unity for this conflicted family is the
meal. The culinary event gathers the family and community, has a
special spirituality, an element that is similar to the eucharist: communion. Hispanics could feel rejected if someone does not eat the
food they have prepared, because their love and soul is in it.

Some women still pray over the food while they are cooking; for
example, while they are preparing the beans, they make a sign of
the cross over the jar of salt, saying: "In the name of God." Also,
"you never eat the first two *tortillas*, because those are for the poor
in thanksgiving to the Divine Providence." Food plays an important role in the Hispanic fiestas or community events. Elvia, a
young leader of Hispanic youth, once said: "Everything else in a
retreat, party or meeting can be wrong or bad, but the food that
gathers us all in a special fraternity and communication has to be
always excellent."

A non-Hispanic priest once asked me how to invite the Hispanic
parishioners to come to communion at Mass, because "Hispanics
do not come to communion if they have not confessed their sins." I
explained to him that his Latino parishioners needed to be taught
about this subject, because for them a sin is a sin, no matter how
grave or venial it may be. They also often have the idea that a family
shares in each of its member's sins. An individual sin can affect the
community, therefore, the common-union. I suggested to him to

invite the Hispanics to communion, not with reflections on what the Law says is right or wrong, but with an appeal that involves feelings, sharing and care: the food.

This is a very general panorama of the history, traditions, religiosity and myths of the largest Hispanic group in the United States: Mexicans. This culture has some things in common with that of other U.S. Latinos, but more research on each particular group is needed. For the present work, this basis is helpful to better understand the people to whom we are going to preach, especially second-generation Hispanics born of a mixture of different contemporary cultures, a new *mestizaje* that is in search of its own identity and expression. I have looked at the older cultural platforms, and now I turn to the new.

GENERATION X

For many, Generation X (GX) is a synonym for confusion and laziness. But this generation has an important message and we need to hear it.

The social atmosphere and the economy of the country have influenced the different generations and the way they look at the world and its future. Demographers use this brief description. "Matures" are those born between the time of the Great Depression and World War II (1929–1945). The "boomers" are the children of the great period of economic progress (1946–1964). Finally, the "GX" are those born between the 1965 stock market crash and the 1976 recession.

Idealism and personal growth seemed to be the characteristics of previous generations, but GX see themselves as determined and ambitious. They enjoy comfort. They like watching TV, from which they get many of their values. They seem to be indifferent to politics. They need to feel close to each other, but without any kind of commitment. They are pragmatic and materialistic and want to create their own way of life. They are cynical about institutions and prefer sarcasm and irony. They also have to deal with diversity: Minority cultures are more assertive in their rights and identity, and in general all have become more aware of multiculturalism, as well as respectful of transgendered persons. They see the future as *mestizo*. "People and their culture perish in isolation, but they are born or reborn in contact with . . . men and women of another culture, another creed, another race" (Carlos Fuentes and Alejandro Escalona, *Chicago Tribune*, Sunday, October 12, 1997, section 2, p. 12). They are a generation of hope. Technology and communications have created links that they think eventually will serve as insurance for a peaceful world. They also have freedom, tolerance and curiosity, which are important elements for peace. These elements, integral to the framework in which Hispanic Generation X has grown, are of special importance for those preaching to this generation.

HISPANIC GENERATION X

The Hispanic GX has taught us how to see the wholeness of the world, to go beyond structures and models, and not to fear the risk of encountering otherness. Their hope for peace and their hunger for community and relationship are key elements that have always been present in Hispanics. In a national Hispanic meeting in Chicago, "Roots and Wings," a young Colombian woman proclaimed to a large audience that her generation wanted to be proud of the roots of their ancestors, but they also wanted to have wings so that they would not feel limited and narrow. She said that she was not only Colombian, but also Mexican, Guatemalan, Irish, Polish, Anglo, Asian, and so on, because of the richness that she had experienced in this country. The same thing happened with a young Mexican American woman who went to Mexico for an international meeting. When she was questioned about why she was there since the meeting was only for Latin Americans, she answered: "I am here because I am representing the country with the second largest number of Hispanics in America and the third largest in the world. So I am representing your people living in the United States in a country that is *mi casa* (my home)" (Elvia B. Torres, *XII Encuentro Latino Americano de Responsables Nacionales de Pastoral Juvenil*, Mexico, D.F. 1997). Rudy Carrasco wrote: "My generation needs to hear a Biblical message: that we are God's children, and our Father considers all that we are—including our race, culture, gender, economic status—

to be valuable. . . . Now throw interracial relationships into the picture—not just the ever-present Latino-White, but Latino-Black and Latino-Asian—and you have an identity crisis fit for the 21st century. Old racial divisions and terminology are dying. We need new words, new models, new dreams, to help us live in a new world. I personally believe that the age-old wisdom of the Bible can affirm my generation in all its complexity, while pointing to a greater, eternal harmony. But will the church be able to communicate this to us?" ("Generation X Latinos," Harambee Christian Family Center, HMC, 1998, 2)

Religion and community are important parts of the world of the Hispanic GX. A significant number of them attend Mass at least once a month, but they are asking for something new: Something that could fulfill their hunger for spirituality, meditation, and an open dialogue between science and religion.

GENERATION "X-SPEAK"

In the NCCHM survey cited earlier, Rosa María Sánchez and I met with young adult professional Hispanics from Los Angeles, Chicago, New York and Miami in order to listen to the different approaches to the Catholic church from them. We were particularly interested in hearing the voices of those who were not practicing their faith.

Concerns about special liturgical and pastoral attention to Hispanic Americans and the progressive confessional changes among them motivated this outreach. NCCHM had discovered that this attention needed to be given especially to the second and third generation. Many of them were professionals who sought to renew and develop their faith and spirituality in order to harmoniously integrate their cultural values with the ethics operative in their lives.

A pilot program for the Evangelization of Hispanic Professionals was designed. The program involved 1. a preliminary planning process and meeting; 2. the identification of a cross-section of Hispanic professionals in every region of the country; 3. a convocation of these professionals for the purpose of articulating their religious concerns and revitalizing their Catholic heritage through a process of dialogue, religious education and service; and 4. a follow-up program.

The results showed that young Hispanics would like to see the church as an instrument of unity. They contend that the Catholic church can support Hispanics in their everyday life by involving them in planning parish events, celebrating the Hispanic cultures and creating an atmosphere of unity and trust. An example given was the organization of social gatherings for the purpose of networking among professionals and their families in church-related activities. They held that the church could also help young Hispanic professionals by bringing together diverse ethnic and socio-economic groups to dialogue as a first step toward a greater understanding of each other, as well as ecumenical meetings to discuss and celebrate our shared religious beliefs. It is clear that young Hispanics want to be included and to participate in their communities by offering their talents and professional skills. They hunger for relationships with different denominations without fear of judgmental attitudes.

They want to be integrated into the decision-making policies affecting Hispanics. They spoke of the need for the church to have outreach programs in the community to welcome Hispanics into the Body of Christ. The Catholic church, they contend, needs to be more welcoming and flexible toward the needs of Hispanics. They also ask for a merciful church, with parish priests who respect the confidentiality of the people who have extended their trust to them. To this end, they explained, the preacher should create an atmosphere of trust, support and confidence in order to build community and to teach that the church is a refuge (home) for everyone, including the Hispanic people.

Young Hispanics specifically asked preachers to better inculturate their preaching by sharing their own struggles. Thus they will be able to see the pastor as a close and real person. They also argued in favor of preaching that is practical and applicable to the daily lives of the parishioners. Preachers, they said, need to be realistic about the problems families face today so that the people in the pews feel understood and supported. Furthermore, they hold that the Catholic church needs to be open in speaking about the struggles of the faithful to live the values that the church teaches. It is also important to share with the people how the clergy as individuals also struggle to live the demands of the gospel.

Young Hispanics also clearly asked that the church help them define Christian values in a complex and alienating world. For example, they asked for help in clarifying the social teaching of the church. They asked for assistance in the development of self-awareness, personal values and spiritual growth. In order to do that, they suggested that they be provided with models of prayer and meditation.

Pastors and priests, they demanded, need to be flexible and open to the people's needs, especially when it comes to receiving the sacraments of baptism and reconciliation. They also challenged those who minister in the Hispanic community to allow Hispanic parishioners to express their own experience in light of the gospel as they interpret it. Thus, preachers need to be open to learning from the self-articulated experience of Hispanic people. This requires attentiveness and an open dialogue with the Hispanic community.

Finally, the young adult Hispanic suggests that parishes need to update the community on how the parish is doing economically, socially and spiritually. They would like to feel welcomed in a familial atmosphere, and to be able to find information about the different activities of the community. They want a continuing dialogue with their church built on trust and mutual respect because they feel that they have much to offer to the ecclesial community. They reject what they perceive to be a list of rules imposed on them, and opt instead for a merciful pastoral outreach. At the same time, they also seek orientation in moral values and spirituality since these are important parts of their lives. Meditation, prayer, love, unification, social justice and ecumenical openness are some of the most important elements that they look for in the Catholic church.

From the preacher, they demand a more creative and dynamic approach using accessible language and practical, realistic examples of families trying to live the fospel. They specifically asked for pedagogical and catechetical preaching that explains the scriptures well, in a language that is simple and accessible. They asked that preachers speak openly and directly to them and their parents on issues that are relevant to the culture in which they live.

They want a church that listens to them and yet guides them toward the spiritual growth that they desire. They want to be joyfully welcomed into the community and given the opportunity to develop their own ideas. They want to be invited to participate in all aspects of parish life. Given that they are often afraid of an uncertain future, they want direction from the church articulated in Christian preaching accessible to them.

In essence, what they are saying is that the young Hispanic Catholics are searching for spiritual leaders who are not afraid to reflect real life in their preaching and to testify in a clear and concrete fashion. And most of all, in moments of confusion and chaos, they ask for something solid: the teaching of the church. Preaching in the Hispanic community must be deeply theological, culturally respectful, easily accessible, personally applicable, rhetorically artful and passionate.

CONCLUSION

For today's preacher, the challenge is not only to learn technique, but also to be genuinely "catholic," that is, open to the inspiration of the Spirit through the people of the Lord. As Jean Macrelis wrote, "Understanding other cultures, possessing multicultural flexibility, may well be today's most important core competency to acquire" ("Understanding Differences in Cultural Communication Styles," *The High School Magazine,* November/December 1997, 30).

The National Conference of Catholic Bishops and the United States Catholic Conference (NCCB/USCC) recognize the importance and the value of the Hispanic presence in the church. They see this presence as a blessing supporting "the growing role Hispanics play in a variety of professional and leadership positions, at all levels of the Church" ("The Hispanic Presence in the Catholic Church in the United States of America," report prepared by Ronaldo M. Cruz, Executive Director of the Secretariat for Hispanic Affairs [Washington: 1997], 1).

Estimates on new waves of Hispanic immigrants force us to consider the future of the Catholic church here in the United States. Presently, we know that "the latest statistical research conducted in the United States about the economic impact of immigrants on the country has revealed that one third of the U.S. population will be

Hispanic by the year 2050. Hispanics will go from 26 to 113 million"
(James P. Smith, research at the Rand Corporation of Santa Monica,
California, presented at Stanford University, 1999). At least sixty percent of them will be Catholics. Although many dioceses have sent
their seminarians to study Spanish, it is very important that future
religious leaders not only speak the language, but also understand
the culture, a culture whose dynamics are in a constant state of
change. It is a tremendous challenge for a minister who wishes to
work within the Hispanic community to approach young Latinos
and Latinas with both a deep respect for their ancestry and an equal
appreciation of their own perspective as *Generación X*.

Preaching must be done from the perspective of the culture that
we would like to evangelize. This is what is called inculturated
evangelization. New challenges are on the horizon because of the
new *mestizaje* formed by the Hispanic Americans who are in the
process of finding their own identity, an identity that continuously
involves both immigration and acculturation. It is especially important that we learn from each new generation and acknowledge their
own expressions of faith, recognize their roots and respect their
process of faith formation. In them I see a mixture of cultures that is
creating a new and challenging area for evangelization. This new
culture combines suffering, pain, low self-esteem, a need for recognition and dignity, adventure, sense of mission, religion, magic,
fiesta and love.

The seeds of the word are incarnated in our new generations but
must also confront each generation. It is the responsibility of the
church's ministers to discover the seeds and cultivate them in order
to help Hispanics harvest and share their own spirituality.

The priest of the small village from southern Mexico who
replaced the Saint James statue could not hear the voice of the
people of God because he did not approach the village with a
missionary attitude of incarnation. He was not interested in their
roots and traditions. He wanted to give them what he thought they
needed. The result was conflict and chaos.

On the other hand, the Guadalupe event teaches us how two
very different cultures can become one. Pope John Paul II has said:
"In America, the *mestiza* face of the Virgin of Guadalupe was from

the start a symbol of the inculturation of the Gospel, of which she has been the lodestar and the guide. Through her powerful intercession, the Gospel will penetrate the hearts of the men and women of America and permeate their cultures, transforming them from within" (*The Church in America*, 70). With Our Lady of Guadalupe, every preacher can find tenderness, compassion, respect, care, faith, passion and love. These are elements that are necessary for the word to be at home among us.

Jorge L. Presmanes, OP

Conclusion: From *Chiles* in the Melting Pot to Saffron in the *Arroz con Pollo*

In our introduction, the metaphor of *chiles* in the melting pot was used to point to the great numbers of Latinos in the church that are dramatically changing its taste. Our contributors have given the Christian preacher a sampling of the myriad flavors that the Hispanic/Latino community adds to the church in North America. From their unique perspectives, they have argued in favor of inculturated preaching as a response to the gift of diversity in the church. Inculturated preaching is not a new concept. Saint Paul championed it 2000 years ago. From its embryonic stages, the church saw as its mission the preaching of the gospel and asserted that its catholicity was found in a common faith in Jesus Christ expressed in the context of a diversity of cultures. The option that the early church made in favor of inculturation required great sacrifice. They had to break with their historical tradition of obedience to the Law as a condition for Christianity.

The cornerstone of the success of the inculturated preaching in the primitive church was an unwavering commitment to proclaiming the gospel matched by an extraordinary openness to the culture of the other. Being in dialogue with the other takes great courage and effort because it requires a willingness to extend one's horizons. But like Saint Paul, the contemporary preacher has no other choice. He or she must be attentive to human experience—not just to assure that the homily is relevant to the assembly, but because the preacher is convinced that the gospel is also encountered and revealed in the midst of the community of believers.

By way of conclusion, there is an issue of importance that needs to be highlighted. To do so, I return to our culinary metaphors. We argued that the culture of the community of the faithful is like the *chile* that adds flavor to the pot. If that is the case, then the preacher is the saffron that adds beauty to the *arroz con pollo*. There is great truth in the maxim "we eat with our eyes first." The thought of sitting down to a plate of colorless *arroz con pollo* is most unappealing. So also is preaching that lacks the color of a calculated gesture or the lively flow of the cadence in which the sermon is delivered. To create a preaching event that is appetizing to the hearer requires imagination, creativity and a profound respect for the art of rhetoric. The important issue of the context and delivery of the sermon is addressed by many homiletics professors who are forming our future preachers. Consideration of their research and insights is invaluable to those of us who seek greater proficiency in the articulation of the Good News.

Finally, we express deep gratitude to our fellow preachers who have stood in pulpits before us and whose ardor for the word sparked our faith in the gospel and our love for preaching. It is because of their passion for this most ancient evangelical art form that we have made Saint Paul's words our own: "Woe to me if I do not preach the gospel."

BIBLIOGRAPHY

Arrastía, Cecilio. *Teoría y Práctica de la Predicación.* Editorial Caribe, 1978.

Brueggemann, Walter. *Cadences of Home: Preaching among Exiles.* Louisville, KY: Westminster Press, 1997.

Costas, Orlando E. *Comunicación Por Medio de la Predicación: Manual de Homilética.* Miami, FL: Editorial Caribe, 1989.

_____. *Liberating News: A Theology of Contextual Evangelization.* Grand Rapids, MI: Eerdmans Publishing Company, 1989.

_____, ed. *Predicación Evangélica y Teología Hispana.* San Diego, CA: Publicaciones de las Américas, 1982.

Cenkner, William, ed. *The Multicultural Church.* New York: Paulist Press, 1996.

Congar, Yves. "Christianity and Faith and Culture." *East Asian Review* 18, no. 4 (1981).

Davis, Kenneth G. "Preaching in Spanish as a Second Language." *Homiletic* 17 (Summer 1992): 7–10.

_____. "When a Bilingual Preacher is Made Not Born." *AIM* (Winter 1999): 18–20.

Elizondo, Virgilio. "The Gospel Unveiled and Proclaimed." In Elizondo, Virgilio P., and Timothy M. Matovina, *San Fernando Cathedral: Soul of the City.* Maryknoll, NY: Orbis Books, 1998.

_____. "Instructions," "Things Encouraged and Discouraged," "Best Answers to Questions," "Goals." In McClure, John S., *Best Advice for Preaching.* Minneapolis, MN: Augsburg Fortress Press, 1998.

Francis, Mark R. *Guidelines for Multicultural Celebrations.* Washington, DC: Federation of Diocesan Liturgical Commissions, 1998.

González, Justo. "Minority Preaching in a Post-Modern Age." In Callen, Barry L., ed., *Sharing Heaven's Music.* Nashville, TN: Abingdon Press, 1995.

González, Justo L., and Catherine G. González. *Liberating Preaching: The Pulpit and the Oppressed.* Nashville, TN: Abingdon Press, 1980.

_____. *The Liberating Pulpit.* Nashville, TN: Abingdon Press, 1994.

Gutiérrez, Angel L., ed. *Voces del Púlpito Hispano.* Valley Forge, PA: Judson Press, 1989.

Hunter, Edwina. "Revisioning the Preaching Curriculum." *Theological Education* (Autumn 1989): 62–84.

Isasi-Diaz, Ada Maria. "By The Rivers of Babylon: Exile as a Way of Life." In Segovia, Fernando F., and Mary Ann Tolbert, eds., *Reading from This Place*. Minneapolis, MN: Fortress Press, 1995, 149–163.

Jiménez, Pablo A. "From Text to Sermon with Philippians 1:1–6: A Hispanic Perspective." *Apuntes* 17, no. 2 (1997): 35–40.

_____, ed. *Lumbrera a Nuestro Camino*. Miami, FL: Editorial Caribe, 1994.

_____. "Predicación y Posmodernidad: Dos Aportes a la Discusión." *Apuntes* 19, no. 1 (1999): 3–7.

Kane, Thomas A. "Forming Global Preachers." *Theological Education* (Autumn 1993): 131–56.

Martinez, Angel. *Operation Wayside and Other Revival Sermons*. Orlando, FL: Christ for the World Publishers, 1966.

Monttesi, Osvaldo L. *Predicación y Misión*. Miami, FL: Logoi, 1989.

Murphy, Frederick J. *Bilingual Homilies for Feast Days and Other Occasions*. Staten Island, NY: Alba House, 1992.

Olmstead, Bob. "Need 'More Preaching' about Jesus." *National Catholic Register* 17 (March 1991): 1, 7.

Pagan, Samuel. *Púlpito, Teología y Esperanza*. Miami, FL: Editorial Caribe, 1988.

Pueblo Publishing Company, Inc. *Homilias Para El Leccionario*. Collegeville, MN: The Liturgical Press, 1990.

Ramírez, Ricardo. "Oyendo Para Entender Las Maravillas de Dios." ¡*Gracias!* 1, nos. 1–2 (January/February 1999, March/April 1999): 3.

_____. "Reflections on the Hispanicization of the Liturgy." *Worship* 57, no. 1 (1983): 26–34.

Rodríguez, Daniel, and Rodolfo Espinosa, eds. *Púlpito Cristiano y Justicia Social*. México: Publicaciones El Faro, 1994.

Rubio, José Antonio. "Interview." *Homily Service*. (April 1997): 27–30.

Segovia, Fernando, and Mary Ann Tolbert, eds. *Readings from This Place: Social Location and Biblical Interpretation*. Minneapolis, MN: Fortress Press, 1995.

Sosa, Juan J. "Renewal and Inculturation." *Liturgy* 9:2 (1990): 17–23.

CONTRIBUTORS

Victor Alvarez, SSP, is the former director of Hispanic ministry for the diocese of Yakima, Washington. He was a staff member of *Familia Cristiana* as well as the national coordinator for vocational orientation for the Mexican province of the Society of St. Paul. He is a former auxiliary member of the National Advisory Pastoral Council to the Mexican bishops. He is currently the director of Hispanic ministry at the University of St. Mary of the Lake in Mundelein, Illinois.

Kenneth G. Davis, OFM CONV, is the director of formation for Hispanic ministry and an assistant professor of pastoral studies at the St. Meinrad School of Theology in St. Meinrad, Indiana.

Raúl Gómez, SDS, is the director of Hispanic studies and an associate professor of pastoral studies at Sacred Heart School of Theology in Hales Corners, Wisconsin. His doctoral dissertation at the Catholic University of America is *Lignum Crucis: The Cross in the Good Friday Celebration of the Hispano-Mozarabic Triduum.*

Rosa María Icaza, CCVI, PHD, is a member of the Congregation of the Sisters of Charity of the Incarnate Word of San Antonio, Texas. She is the associate director of the programs department at the Mexican-American Cultural Center in San Antonio, Texas. She received her doctorate from the Catholic University of America in Washington. She has been a member of the Sub-Committee for Hispanic Liturgy of the Bishops' Committee for the Liturgy since 1981. She was president of the *Instituto de Liturgia Hispana* and an ex-officio member of BCL from 1988 to 1994. She is widely published and is currently finishing a new bilingual publication: *Quinceañera: Celebration of Life. A Guidebook for Presiders of the Religious Rite.*

María Luisa Iglesias, SC, is a Sister of Charity of New York. She has been with RENEW International since 1990 and is currently the coordinator of the Hispanic team.

Jaime Lara, PhD, is a priest of the diocese of Brooklyn, New York, assistant professor of Christian art and architecture, and adjunct professor of liturgics at Yale University Divinity School. His most recent work is *City, Temple, Stage: Architecture, Eschatology, and Evangelism in Colonial Mexico.*

Jorge Presmanes, OP, is the pastor of St. Dominic Church, a predominantly Latino Catholic parish in Miami, Florida. He is a graduate of the Dominican School at the Graduate Theological Union in Berkeley, California. He is currently a candidate for a doctorate in ministry at Barry University in Miami. He also teaches at the Southeast Pastoral Institute and is the promoter of Hispanic ministries for the Southern Dominican Province.

Juan Sosa is a priest of the archdiocese of Miami, Florida. He has served the archdiocese as associate director of religious education, co-director of the permanent diaconate program and, currently, as executive director of the ministry of worship and spiritual life. He is currently the pastor of St. Catherine of Siena Church. He has recently published his first book *Cultos, Sectas y Sincretismos* to assist pastoral agents throughout the country with the various religious manifestations prevalent among Hispanic Catholics. He is a former president of the *Instituto de Liturgia Hispana* and is currently a member of the BCL Sub-Committee for Hispanic Liturgy.